RISE AND SHINE: A WOMAN'S BLUEPRINT FOR HIGH SELF-ESTEEM

EMBRACING YOUR INNER STRENGTH AND CULTIVATING SELF-WORTH IN A SOCIAL WORLD

DANIEL POWERS

TABLE OF CONTENTS

INTRODUCTION

There once was a time when Sarah, a vibrant and seemingly confident woman, found herself caught in the shadows of self-doubt and comparison. Despite her accomplishments and the love surrounding her, Sarah's reflection in the mirror was often met with criticism rather than kindness. Her journey from this place of uncertainty to one of self-love and unwavering confidence is a testament to the transformative power of high self-esteem. It's a journey that many of us are familiar with and the very essence of what we will explore together in this book.

"Rise and Shine: A Woman's Blueprint for High Self-Esteem" is more than just a title; it's a mission. This book is crafted to help you, dear reader, discover and embrace your inner strength, elevate your self-esteem, and thrive in a world that often bombards us with unrealistic standards and expectations. At its core, it is a guide for navigating the complexities of today's social landscape with grace and confidence, recognizing your worth, and radiating your true self.

In our current context, where social media and societal pressures constantly shape our perceptions of self-worth, self-esteem has never been more crucial. Statistics and studies from leading psychologists highlight a troubling trend: a growing number of women battle with low self-esteem, influenced by an ever-elusive standard of perfection. This book seeks to address this pervasive issue head-on, offering you a lifeline in the form of stories, expert advice, and, most importantly, practical, real-world solutions.

Structured to take you on a transformative journey, "Rise and Shine" is divided into carefully curated chapters, each designed to build upon the last, guiding you from self-discovery to self-love and beyond. Along the way, you'll find engaging exercises, reflective questions, and actionable steps that encourage you to engage deeply with the content, tailoring this journey to your own unique experience.

But this book is more than a solitary journey; it's an invitation to join a community of like-minded women who are all embarking on their paths to high self-esteem. Together, this forms a network of support and encouragement, a collective force of empowerment and change.

As we stand at the threshold of this journey, I invite you to step forward with hope and enthusiasm. Let this book be your guide, your companion, and your inspiration as you embark on the transformative path toward embracing your true worth. The time to rise and shine is now, and it starts with the simple yet profound act of opening these pages and daring to believe in the power of your own self-esteem.

Together, let's take that first step.

THE FOUNDATION OF SELF-ESTEEM

I n the quiet moments before dawn, when the world seems to hold its breath in anticipation of the new day, a solitary figure stands before a mirror. This daily ritual, often overlooked in the hustle of morning routines, is where the battle for self-esteem begins. Here, in the reflection, lies not just the image of a person but the embodiment of their self-worth, their inner narrative, and the complex interplay of history, biology, and culture that shapes their perception of self.

THE ROOTS OF SELF-ESTEEM: UNDERSTANDING ITS POWER

At its core, self-esteem is the appraisal of one's worth. It's the silent whisper that narrates our ability to face the day, assert our needs, and pursue our desires. It's both the shield against the slings and arrows of life's challenges and the sword with which we carve out our path. It is, without hyperbole, the foundation upon which our mental health and overall well-being are built. The American Psychological Association highlights self-esteem's critical role in our lives, evidencing its influence on life choices, relationships, and personal fulfillment.

The journey of understanding self-esteem's power is not a recent phenomenon. Historically, philosophers, from the stoics of ancient Greece to the existentialists of the 20th century, grappled with concepts of self-worth and individual purpose. In the 18th century, David Hume spoke of the self as a bundle of perceptions, laying early groundwork for understanding the fluid nature of self-esteem. Fast forward to the modern era, where psychologist William James, in the late 19th century, introduced one of the earliest formal theories on self-esteem, suggesting it results from the ratio of our achievements to our expectations. This historical exploration reveals a fascinating evolution of thought, from the philosophical to the psychological, all converging on the understanding that self-esteem is pivotal to the human experience.

Delving deeper, the biology of belief unveils the neurological underpinnings of self-esteem. Neuroscience has laid bare the neural pathways that light up in response to positive self-affirmation. Regions such as the ventromedial prefrontal cortex become active when we engage in positive self-reflection, according to research published in the journal "Social Cognitive and Affective Neuroscience." This biological basis offers insight and hope: the understanding that through deliberate practice, we can rewire our brains for positive self-perception, a concept known as neuroplasticity. This ability to shape our neural pathways underscores the dynamic nature of self-esteem; it is not a fixed trait but a malleable quality that can be cultivated.

Culture, in its myriad forms, plays a significant role in shaping our understanding and valuation of self-esteem. Across the globe, the perception of self-worth varies dramatically, influenced by societal norms, collective values, and historical context. In individualistic societies like the United States, self-esteem often hinges on personal achievement and independence. Contrast this with collectivist cultures, where harmony, community, and interdependence are valued, and self-esteem is more closely tied to social roles and relationships. These cultural influences offer a lens through which to view self-esteem not just as a personal journey but as a reflection of the larger tapestry of human society.

Reflective Exercise: Mapping Your Self-Esteem Landscape

Take a moment to reflect on your self-esteem landscape. Consider the following prompts to guide your reflection:

- **Historical Influences**: Can you identify any historical or philosophical influences on your personal beliefs about self-worth? Consider family narratives, educational experiences, or significant life events that have shaped your perception of self-esteem.
- **Biological Awareness**: Reflect on moments when you've experienced a strong sense of self-worth. What physical sensations accompanied these moments? Acknowledging self-esteem's biological aspect can heighten our awareness of its presence in our lives.
- **Cultural Context**: How has your cultural background influenced your understanding of self-esteem? Identify specific cultural beliefs, practices, or values that have impacted your sense of self-worth.

This exercise invites us to delve into the complexities of self-esteem, recognize its roots in our lives, and begin cultivating a deeper, more resilient sense of self.

Our reflections on self-esteem, informed by the intricate dance of history, biology, and culture, reveal the multifaceted nature of this essential aspect of our being. As we navigate the following chapters, remember that understanding self-esteem's roots is the first step in harnessing its power to rise and shine in every facet of our lives.

REWRITING YOUR SELF-ESTEEM STORY: FROM PAST TO PRESENT

In the tapestry of our lives, the threads of past narratives often weave a complex pattern, shaping the fabric of our self-esteem. These stories, etched into the very core of our being, narrate tales of triumphs and defeats, love and loss, shaping our self-view in profound ways. Yet, amid this intricately woven narrative lies the power of transformation, the ability to reframe and redefine the essence of our self-esteem. The journey begins with recognizing these narratives and acknowledging their presence and influence on our self-perception.

Identifying negative narratives demands a pause, a moment of introspection where we listen to the stories we tell ourselves. In the quiet reflection, one might hear the echoes of "not good enough," "unworthy," or "incapable," reverberating through their thoughts. Often rooted in past experiences, these narratives hold sway over our present, casting long shadows over our potential. Recognition becomes the first step towards liberation, a beacon of awareness in the murky waters of self-doubt.

Enter the realm of narrative therapy, a beacon of hope in the quest for self-esteem transformation. This therapeutic approach operates on a foundational belief: we are not merely subjects in our life stories but the authors. Narrative therapy empowers individuals to separate themselves from their problems, viewing these issues as external entities rather than intrinsic characteristics. Through techniques such as externalization, individuals learn to re-author their stories, transforming narratives of self-doubt into tales of resilience and strength. It's akin to editing a manuscript, where each revision brings clarity, perspective, and a renewed sense of agency.

The stories of public figures who have navigated the tumultuous seas of self-esteem offer inspiration and insight. Consider the narrative of a well-known athlete, once plagued by self-doubt, who rose to achieve global recognition. Or the tale of a celebrated author who, despite countless rejections, persevered to pen bestsellers. These stories resonate not because of their fairy-tale endings but because of their authenticity, their testament to the human capacity for growth and change. They serve as reminders that the transformation of self-esteem is not only possible but within reach.

Actionable steps for rewriting our self-esteem narratives beckon us toward practical application. The journey from recognition to transformation is personal and unique yet grounded in universal principles guiding the way. Begin with the writing of your current narrative, a raw, unfiltered account of the stories you tell yourself. This act of writing serves as a mirror, reflecting the contours of your self-esteem landscape.

Next, engage in the practice of externalization. Name your struggles, be it "The Critic," "The Doubter," or "The Perfectionist." In doing so, you create a distinct entity, one that is separate from your essence. This separation is crucial, for it shifts the battlefield, allowing you to confront these challenges not as inherent flaws but as external adversaries.

Armed with this perspective, embark on the process of re-authoring. This stage invites creativity, weaving new narratives that champion your strengths, resilience, and achievements. Identify moments of triumph, no matter how small, and incorporate them into your story. These instances serve as pillars, supporting a narrative of empowerment and self-belief.

Integrate the tales of role models who inspire you, drawing parallels between their journey and your own. Their stories become a canvas upon which you can project your aspirations, a source of motivation, and a roadmap to self-esteem transformation.

Finally, letter writing is a powerful tool in the rewriting process. Write a letter to your future self, one that embodies your highest aspirations and self-esteem. Conversely, write to your past self, offering compassion, understanding, and the wisdom of hindsight. These letters are tangible artifacts of your commitment to growth, a dialogue between who you were, who you are, and who you aspire to be.

The rewriting of our self-esteem narratives is not a journey embarked upon lightly. It demands courage, introspection, and a steadfast commitment to growth. Yet, within this process, we discover not only the power of our stories but the strength within ourselves to transform them. The past, with its shadows and echoes, need not dictate the contours of our self-esteem. Instead, armed with awareness, therapeutic insights, and actionable strategies, we possess the tools to reframe our narratives to step into the light of self-acceptance and unwavering confidence.

THE SELF-ESTEEM MIRROR: REFLECTIONS ON OUR SELF-PERCEPTION

In the solitude of our most reflective moments, the mirror before us serves not merely as a reflector of physical form but as a portal into the depths of our self-perception. This "self-esteem mirror" holds up not just the image of our external selves but a complex vista of our internal narratives, beliefs, and the emotions that color our view of who we are. Its surface, seemingly smooth, is often rippled with the undercurrents of our deepest feelings about ourselves—each reflection a tapestry of our triumphs, insecurities, aspirations, and fears.

Yet, the integrity of this mirror is perpetually at risk of distortion, its clarity muddied by the relentless barrage of external factors that insidiously influence our self-view. With its relentless onslaught of images depicting idealized forms of beauty and success, the media erects a facade of perfection that is as pervasive as it is unattainable. The comparison, that insidious thief of joy, further skews our perception as we measure our worth against the meticulously curated lives of peers, forgetting that what glimmers on the surface often belies the complexity beneath.

Clearing the fog from our self-esteem mirror is both necessary and challenging, requiring a deliberate effort to peel away the layers of distortion and gaze upon our true selves with clarity and kindness. Strategies for achieving this clarity begin with a conscious disengagement from the sources of distortion. Limiting exposure to media that fuels unrealistic standards of beauty and success and fostering an awareness of the curated nature of social media can help mitigate the relentless pressure to compare and conform.

Simultaneously, the cultivation of self-compassion emerges as a powerful antidote to the harsh judgments we often impose upon ourselves. Recognizing our common humanity, that we are not alone in our struggles or imperfections, fosters a sense of connectedness and empathy towards ourselves. Engaging in positive self-talk, a nurturing and forgiving dialogue, acts as a balm, soothing the wounds inflicted by criticism and comparison. This practice of self-compassion, rooted in kindness and understanding, gradually restores the integrity of our self-esteem mirror, allowing us to view ourselves with a gentler, more accepting gaze.

Practicing self-reflection, the deliberate introspection into our thoughts, feelings, and behaviors, further polishes the mirror of our self-esteem. This reflective practice, whether through journaling, meditation, or mindfulness, encourages a deeper exploration of our internal landscape. It invites us to question the narratives we hold about ourselves, distinguishing the voice of our inner critic from the truth of our inherent worth. Through self-reflection, we learn to recognize our strengths, acknowledge our achievements, and accept our flaws not as failings but as facets of our unique human experience.

In this reflective process, we also discover the power of reframing our experiences. Challenges and setbacks, rather than evidence of inadequacy, become opportunities for growth and learning. Successes and triumphs, no matter how small, are celebrated as affirmations of our capabilities and resilience. This shift in perspective, from a focus on deficiency to one of abundance, transforms the self-esteem mirror from a source of self-critique to a reflection of self-appreciation.

As we engage in these practices, the mirror of our self-esteem gradually clears, revealing not a flawless specimen but a beautifully complex individual worthy of love and respect. This clearer, kinder reflection becomes a source of strength and confidence, a reminder of our inherent worth beyond the superficial judgments of society. By clearing the fog from our self-esteem mirror, we reclaim the power to define ourselves on our own terms, recognize our worth, and reflect the light of our true selves into the world.

CULTIVATING A SELF-ESTEEM GARDEN: DAILY PRACTICES FOR GROWTH

Moments spent in reflection and self-care in the quiet predawn or solitude of evening sow the seeds of a robust self-esteem garden. This cultivation demands consistency, a daily commitment to practices that water the soil of our being with kindness and nurture the growth of our inner worth. The rituals we adopt, simple yet profound, become the sunlight and rain on our burgeoning self-esteem.

Daily Rituals

Morning affirmations, whispered in the soft light of dawn, act as the first rays of the sun, illuminating the possibilities of the day ahead. These positive and personal affirmations anchor us in a mindset of self-acceptance and potential. Similarly, an evening gratitude practice, where the day's blessings are recounted, serves to water the garden of our self-esteem, reminding us of our capabilities and achievements, even in the face of adversity. Between the bookends of day and night, moments stolen for deep breathing or mindful pauses act as the nutrients that enrich our self-perception, grounding us in the present and fortifying us against the erosion of doubt.

The Role of Self-Care

Self-care practices, often misconstrued as indulgent, are the compost that enriches the soil of our self-esteem garden. Regular physical activity, whether a brisk walk under the canopy of trees or a series of stretches in the warmth of sunlight, strengthens the body and mind, reinforcing our sense of agency and self-efficacy. Nutrition, too, plays a crucial role; meals prepared and consumed with mindfulness nourish the body and, by extension, our self-worth, reminding us of the importance of self-nurturance. Sleep, that most elusive yet essential restorative, acts as the moonlight under which our self-esteem garden quietly flourishes, healing the wear and tear of daily life.

Growth Mindset

Adopting a growth mindset, where challenges are seen not as insurmountable walls but as fertile ground for development, is pivotal. This mindset, characterized by a belief in the potential for growth and learning, is the soil in which the seeds of high self-esteem are planted. It encourages us to view setbacks as opportunities for germination, where new strengths can sprout, and existing ones can be fortified. A growth mindset thrives on feedback, using it as the compost that enriches our understanding and skills rather than as the frost that withers our confidence.

In this fertile soil, failures transform into the roots of resilience, delving deep into the earth, stabilizing and nourishing us. Successes, on the other hand, blossom into flowers, their colors a vivid reminder of our capabilities and worth. Together, they create a balanced ecosystem where self-esteem can flourish, resistant to the droughts of criticism and the pests of comparison.

Community Gardening

No garden, however well-tended, exists in isolation. The support of a community, a collective of fellow gardeners, provides a protective canopy under which individual self-esteem gardens can thrive. These communities, whether forged in the physical realm or knit together in the digital ether, offer sunlight and shelter. They provide a space for sharing growth tips, celebrating blooms, and commiserating over losses. Here, the wisdom of those who have cultivated their gardens through seasons of joy and hardship becomes a beacon, guiding us through foggy mornings and stormy nights.

In these communities, vulnerability and strength coexist, and showing one's true self, complete with imperfections and scars, is not just accepted but celebrated. Nurturing others' self-esteem gardens through encouragement, empathy, and shared experiences inadvertently strengthens our own. This reciprocal cultivation creates a lush landscape where diverse gardens of self-esteem, each unique in its beauty and resilience, stand as a testament to the collective power of support and solidarity.

In this ongoing cultivation process, where daily self-care rituals and mindful reflection mingle with the adoption of a growth mindset and the nurturing embrace of community, our self-esteem gardens flourish. They become resilient oases of self-worth, where the fruits of our labor—confidence, resilience, and a profound sense of self-acceptance—nourish us, enabling us to face the world with hope and a deep-rooted belief in our own value.

THE SOCIAL FABRIC OF SELF-ESTEEM

In the quiet predawn hours, beneath the soft glow of the kitchen light, a mother carefully prepares breakfast. Each plate is filled with nourishment and love, a daily ritual that weaves the fabric of family life. Here, in these everyday moments, the threads of self-esteem are delicately spun, each interaction a stitch in the tapestry of our self-worth. The family, that first society we encounter, holds the loom on which our perceptions of self are intricately woven. Within this intimate constellation, our foundational beliefs about who we are and what we can become take root.

THE FAMILY TAPESTRY: UNTANGLING SELF-ESTEEM THREADS

Family Dynamics

From the earliest moments of life, the family environment begins to mold our self-esteem. Here, in the echoes of parental voices and the reflections seen in the eyes of siblings, we first perceive our value. Positive affirmations and supportive feedback from family members are fertile soil for healthy self-esteem to grow. Conversely, criticism and neglect plant seeds of doubt that can shadow our self-view for years. Understanding this dynamic reveals the profound influence family has on shaping our self-esteem, setting the stage for engaging with the world beyond the family unit.

Breaking Free from Negative Influences

Not all family tapestries are woven with threads of support and encouragement. Some bear the marks of criticism, neglect, or unrealistic expectations, patterns that can entangle our self-esteem. To untangle these threads requires recognition and resilience. Recognizing the source of these negative influences is the first step, akin to identifying the weeds in a garden before they can be removed. Strategies such as setting healthy boundaries and seeking external support from friends, mentors, or professionals can aid this process. It involves a delicate balance of acknowledging the impact of one's upbringing while asserting autonomy over one's self-esteem narrative.

Fostering Positive Relationships

Cultivating positive family relationships is akin to tending a garden, requiring patience, effort, and the understanding that growth takes time. Open communication is the sunlight under which these relationships flourish, illuminating the needs and feelings of each member. Regular family meetings, where each voice is heard and valued, can strengthen the ties that bind, enriching the soil of collective self-esteem. Celebrating individual and family achievements, respecting differences, and supporting one another through challenges are the nutrients that feed this growth, fostering an environment where self-esteem can thrive.

Creating Your Chosen Family

Not all who wander the path of self-esteem do so with the support of their biological family. For some, the concept of a chosen family offers a beacon of hope. This chosen family, formed from friends, mentors, and companions who share our values and support our growth, becomes an essential support network. They are the people who mirror our worth back to us when we cannot see it ourselves, the collective embrace that holds us during times of doubt. Engaging with communities based on shared interests, goals, or experiences can provide a sense of belonging and validation crucial for nurturing self-esteem. Choosing those we consider family reaffirms our agency in shaping our self-esteem landscape.

Visual Element: Interactive Family Dynamics Chart

An interactive chart allows readers to map their family dynamics, identifying sources of support and areas of conflict affecting their self-esteem. Through a series of prompts and questions, this tool facilitates a deeper understanding of family relationships and their impact on self-worth.

1. **List family members and their relationship to you**: Start by listing each family member and your relationship to them (e.g., mother, father, sibling).
2. **Identify types of interactions**: For each family member, note the kinds of interactions you have (positive, negative, neutral) and the frequency.
3. **Reflect on impact**: Reflect on how each relationship impacts your self-esteem. Consider which relationships provide support and which may require boundary-setting.
4. **Action plan**: Based on your reflections, create an action plan to enhance positive relationships and address or

mitigate negative ones.

This exercise, grounded in the reality of family dynamics, offers a structured approach to untangling the complex web of relationships that shape our self-esteem. It emphasizes the importance of proactive engagement in fostering supportive networks, whether biological or chosen, as a cornerstone of self-esteem development.

In the intricate dance of family life, where each interaction holds the potential to weave threads of confidence or sow seeds of doubt, understanding the profound impact of these dynamics is crucial. As we navigate the complexities of these relationships, the goal remains clear: to cultivate a tapestry of self-esteem that is rich, resilient, and reflective of our inherent worth.

SOCIAL MEDIA AND SELF-WORTH: NAVIGATING THE DOUBLE-EDGED SWORD

In an era where the digital landscape forms the backdrop of our daily interactions, social media emerges as both a sanctuary and a battleground for self-esteem. This dichotomy, inherent in its design, invites users into a world of endless connection, yet it is within this world that the fabric of our self-worth can become frayed. The relationship between social media use and self-esteem is not linear but a complex weave of influence, where validation and comparison engage in a continuous dance. Each like, comment, and share carries the weight of approval, yet beneath this surface of interaction lurks the shadow of comparison, a silent thief of joy. Studies have shown a correlation between excessive social media use and diminished self-esteem, pointing to the pervasive culture of comparison as a primary culprit. However, this relationship is flexible but malleable, subject to how we engage with these digital platforms.

Curating a positive online experience becomes crucial in wielding social media to enhance, rather than diminish, self-worth. This curation involves a conscious selection of content that uplifts and inspires, deliberately filtering the digital stream that flows into our lives. It begins with auditing our social media feeds and critically examining the accounts we follow and consume content. Accounts that foster negativity or elicit feelings of inadequacy are pruned, making room for those that celebrate authenticity, positivity, and real human connection. Additionally, the implementation of screen-time tools offered by many platforms aids in this curation process, allowing for a measured engagement that respects the boundaries of our mental well-being.

Creating authentic connections online transcends the superficial interactions that often characterize social media. It involves a shift from passive consumption to active engagement, where the digital space becomes a conduit for meaningful interaction. Strategies for fostering these connections include:

- Sharing content that reflects our true selves.
- Engaging in conversations that move beyond the superficial.
- Seeking out communities aligned with our values and interests.

These communities, centered around hobbies, causes, or mutual support, offer a sense of belonging that can bolster self-esteem. They remind us that we share common hopes, struggles, and dreams beneath the curated facades. Authenticity becomes the currency of these interactions, a shared language that deepens connections and nurtures self-worth.

Yet, even in the most carefully curated digital environment, the need for detoxification and boundary-setting becomes evident. The constant influx of information, the relentless demand for attention, and the pervasive culture of comparison can lead to digital fatigue. In this state, social media ceases to be a source of joy and connection and becomes a drain on our mental resources. Recognizing the signs of digital fatigue is the first step in addressing its impact on our self-esteem. These signs may manifest as feelings of inadequacy, jealousy, or disconnection from oneself and others. The decision to detox and step back from social media is personal, yet it is grounded in the recognition that our well-being takes precedence over digital engagement.

Guidance on when and how to take breaks from social media is not prescriptive but relatively intuitive, a reflection of our unique needs and circumstances. It might involve designated periods of disconnection, where digital devices are set aside in favor of real-world interactions and experiences. Alternatively, it might mean reducing social media use and consciously deciding to engage less frequently or less intensively. During these periods of detoxification, the cultivation of offline interests and activities becomes paramount. Pursuits that engage the mind and body, whether creative endeavors, physical activity, or simply the enjoyment of nature, can replenish the mental and emotional reserves depleted by excessive digital consumption. In this way, detoxification becomes not just a retreat from the digital but an embrace of the tangible, a reconnection with the immediate and the real.

Navigating the double-edged sword of social media and self-worth demands a nuanced approach, an understanding that while these platforms can challenge our self-esteem, they also hold the potential for connection, inspiration, and self-expression. The key lies in conscious engagement, in curating our digital experiences to reflect our values and uplift our spirits. It involves forging genuine connections in a realm often criticized for its superficiality and recognizing when to step back, detox, and reconnect with ourselves and the world around us. In this careful balancing act, we find a path through the digital landscape that enhances rather than diminishes our self-worth. This path leads not to comparison and inadequacy but to authenticity and connection.

FRIENDSHIP'S INFLUENCE: THE COMPANY WE KEEP AND OUR SELF-ESTEEM

In the intricate web of human interaction, friendships stand as pivotal structures, their architecture built on shared experiences, mutual respect, and the profound impact they wield on our self-perception. Therefore, choosing friends becomes a critical endeavor, akin to selecting the beams that will support the edifice of our self-esteem. Friends who uplift and champion our worth act as sturdy pillars, reinforcing the foundation of our confidence, while those who erode our sense of self through negativity or indifference can undermine the very structure we rely on for emotional shelter.

Discerning friendships that enrich our lives requires a reflective analysis, a mindful evaluation of the qualities we value in companionship, and the reciprocal nature of support and respect. Friends who encourage our aspirations, empathize with our vulnerabilities, and celebrate our achievements without reservation are treasures. They mirror the best versions of ourselves, reflecting the strength and potential we may not always see. The presence of such individuals in our lives acts as a catalyst for growth, inspiring us to reach higher, knowing we have a safety net of encouragement and support.

Conversely, the landscape of human relationships is sometimes marred by connections that drain rather than nourish our spirits. Toxic friendships, characterized by patterns of manipulation, jealousy, or chronic negativity, can insidiously erode our self-esteem. Identifying these harmful dynamics necessitates a keen awareness of our emotional responses to interactions and an attunement to feelings of discomfort, inadequacy, or guilt that may signal an imbalance in the relationship. The courage to address these concerns directly, to set boundaries or, if necessary, to sever ties, is an act of self-preservation. It reaffirms our right to emotional well-being and the importance of surrounding ourselves with individuals who respect and uplift us.

Forming healthy friendships, those towers of mutual respect and genuine affection are intentional. It begins with laying a foundation built on authenticity, the courage to present our true selves, imperfections included. This vulnerability, far from a weakness, is the mortar that binds, creating connections rooted in honesty and trust. Communication, too, is critical, a two-way street where thoughts and feelings are exchanged with the assurance of being heard and valued. Active listening, empathy, and the willingness to negotiate and compromise further strengthen these bonds, creating a resilient structure capable of weathering the storms of life.

Yet, the fabric of friendship is not static but dynamic, requiring ongoing maintenance and nurturing. Regular check-ins, sharing experiences, and the simple act of showing up, whether in moments of celebration or in times of need, keep the connection vibrant and strong. Celebrating each other's successes without competition or envy fosters an environment where self-esteem can flourish. Additionally, acknowledging and resolving conflicts, approached with an open heart and a willingness to understand, ensure that minor rifts do not widen into irreparable breaches.

At the heart of friendship lies the principle of reciprocity, a mutual exchange of support and esteem that elevates all involved. This reciprocal nature underscores the profound impact friendships have on our self-perception. In giving of ourselves, in offering support, empathy, and encouragement, we not only bolster the self-esteem of our friends but reinforce our own sense of worth. The act of helping a friend navigate challenges, of being a source of strength and comfort, reaffirms our capabilities and value. Simultaneously, receiving support and feeling seen and understood roots us more deeply in knowing our worth.

Therefore, friendship's influence on our self-esteem cannot be overstated. When rooted in mutual respect, empathy, and support, these connections act as mirrors reflecting our best selves. They remind us of our worth, encourage our growth, and provide a sanctuary of understanding and acceptance. In the company we keep, we find not just companions for the journey but architects of our self-esteem, individuals who, through their presence, help construct the strongest version of ourselves.

ROMANTIC RELATIONSHIPS: LOVE'S REFLECTION ON OUR SELF-WORTH

In the intricate dance of human connection, romantic relationships often serve as both mirrors and molders of our self-esteem, reflecting deeply held beliefs about our worthiness of love and affection. The interplay between self-esteem and the selection of romantic partners is nuanced, rooted in the subconscious patterns that guide us toward or away from specific individuals. Within this context, our self-esteem can flourish in the warmth of mutual respect and love or wither under the cold shadow of neglect and criticism.

The influence of self-esteem on our romantic choices is profound, acting as an invisible hand that steers us toward partners who resonate with our deepest perceptions of self. High self-esteem attracts nurturing and balanced relationships where mutual respect and support are given freely. Conversely, low self-esteem might draw us into dynamics where our needs and boundaries are overlooked or dismissed, mirroring back to us our hidden fears and doubts about our intrinsic value. This magnetic pull towards partners who reflect our self-esteem level underscores the importance of nurturing our self-worth, ensuring that it is rooted in a healthy, loving acceptance of ourselves.

Distinguishing between relationships that nourish self-esteem and those that deplete it involves a keen awareness of their characteristics. Relationships fostering growth and happiness share common features such as open communication, mutual support, and celebrating each other's successes without jealousy or competition. In these unions, challenges are navigated with empathy and understanding, and individuality is cherished rather than suppressed. In stark contrast, relationships detrimental to self-esteem often suffer from chronic criticism, lack of trust, and an imbalance of power where one partner's needs dominate the narrative. Recognizing these signs enables individuals to make informed choices about their romantic involvements, prioritizing their emotional well-being.

Maintaining a robust sense of self within a romantic relationship requires deliberate effort and mindfulness. It involves carving out space for personal growth, hobbies, and friendships outside the partnership, ensuring one's identity remains intact and vibrant. Regular self-reflection and open dialogue about needs and boundaries help preserve individuality, while shared goals and dreams foster a sense of partnership and mutual respect. This balanced approach allows love to be a source of empowerment rather than a constraint, enhancing self-esteem by affirming one's worth.

While often laden with sorrow, the conclusion of a romantic relationship holds invaluable lessons about self-worth and personal growth. These endings, painful as they may be, offer an opportunity to reflect on the relationship dynamics, our role within them, and the aspects of ourselves that were illuminated or overshadowed by the partnership. This period of reflection can pave the way for healing, allowing us to emerge with a deeper understanding of our needs, desires, and the non-negotiable aspects of our self-esteem. It teaches resilience, the capacity to recover and rebuild, reinforcing the knowledge that our worth is not contingent upon another's presence or approval.

The intertwined nature of love and self-esteem becomes evident in navigating the complex waters of romantic relationships. These connections, in their most nurturing form, act as mirrors reflecting our worthiness of love and respect. They remind us that at the heart of every romantic endeavor lies the opportunity for growth, deepening our understanding of ourselves and the boundless capacity of the human heart to love and be loved. As we move forward, let us carry with us the lessons learned from loves past and present, allowing them to inform and enrich our journeys toward a self-esteem that is resilient, vibrant, and deeply rooted in self-love. This foundation of self-worth enhances our romantic connections and enriches every aspect of our lives, paving the way for relationships that uplift, inspire, and affirm our inherent value.

As we transition from exploring romantic relationships and their impact on self-esteem, we carry forward the understanding that our worth is reflected in and shaped by the connections we choose to nurture. This realization underscores the importance of cultivating a robust sense of self-worth, one that guides us toward relationships that honor and celebrate our true selves. In the chapters that follow, we will delve deeper into the practices and mindsets that fortify our self-esteem, ensuring that it becomes a wellspring of strength and joy in our lives.

SELF-CARE AS A FOUNDATION

I magine standing in a lush garden at dawn, the first light of day caressing the dew-kissed petals of blooming flowers. This garden did not flourish overnight; it required time, attention, and various nurturing practices. Similarly, self-care is the garden of our well-being, a multifaceted cultivation that extends far beyond the simplistic notions of pampering. It is an intricate blend of actions and decisions, each contributing to the flourishing of our mental, physical, and emotional health.

THE SELF-CARE SPECTRUM: BEYOND BUBBLE BATHS

Expanding the Definition

Self-care, often encapsulated in images of bubble baths and spa days, holds a much richer tapestry of practices encompassing the entirety of our being. From the food we consume to the boundaries we set with others, each aspect of self-care contributes to a holistic sense of well-being. It's akin to the multifaceted care a gardener bestows upon their garden, understanding that water alone does not suffice—there must also be sunlight, pruning, and nutrient-rich soil. Similarly, self-care spans physical activities, mental breaks, emotional expression, and spiritual practices, each tailored to meet individual needs and circumstances.

Self-Care vs. Self-Indulgence

The line between self-care and self-indulgence blurs when temporary pleasures are mistaken for acts of genuine care. While indulging in a decadent dessert or a shopping spree may offer immediate gratification, they do not necessarily address deeper needs for rest, connection, or self-esteem. Proper self-care sometimes involves making difficult choices for long-term well-being, such as choosing a night of rest over a late social event or opting for a nutritious meal over fast food. It requires discernment to recognize what truly nourishes us versus what momentarily satiates.

Accessibility of Self-Care

In a world where self-care is commercialized, it's crucial to underscore its accessibility to people from all walks of life. Self-care need not entail costly services or products; it can be as simple as taking a moment to breathe deeply, stepping outside to feel the sun on your face, or setting aside time to connect with a loved one. It's the democratization of well-being, understanding that the essence of self-care lies in its adaptability to our unique lives and resources.

Integrating Self-Care into Daily Life

Integrating self-care into daily life is akin to weaving a safety net that catches us in moments of stress or fatigue. It begins with small, manageable actions—a five-minute morning stretch, a nightly gratitude journal, or a midday walk. Consider the practice of scheduling short breaks throughout the workday, not as lost time but as essential moments to recharge, enhancing productivity and creativity.

Visual Element: Self-Care Wheel

A Self-Care Wheel, divided into Physical, Emotional, Social, Spiritual, Intellectual, and Professional segments, offers a visual representation of the breadth of self-care practices. For each segment, suggestions tailored to various lifestyles and resources encourage readers to identify and incorporate practices into their routines. For instance, under the Physical segment, options range from a structured workout to a dance break in the living room. This wheel serves as a reminder of the diverse avenues through which we can nurture ourselves.

Reflective Exercise: Crafting Your Self-Care Plan

1. **Identify Needs**: Begin by reflecting on areas of your life that feel neglected or strained. Is it physical exhaustion, emotional turmoil, or perhaps a lack of intellectual stimulation?
2. **Choose Practices**: Refer to the Self-Care Wheel to select practices that address these needs. Aim for variety, considering activities that nourish different aspects of your well-being.
3. **Set Realistic Goals**: Set achievable goals for each chosen practice. If meditation is your chosen practice, start with three minutes daily and gradually increase the time.
4. **Create a Schedule**: Integrate these practices into your daily routine, assigning specific times for each. Treating self-care as a non-negotiable appointment increases the likelihood of adherence.
5. **Evaluate and Adjust**: Regularly assess the effectiveness of your self-care plan. Be open to making adjustments,

recognizing that your needs may evolve over time.

This exercise underscores the importance of intentionality in self-care, encouraging a proactive approach to structured and flexible well-being.

In the garden of well-being, self-care stands as the sun, water, and soil that nurture our growth. It is a spectrum that encompasses a wide array of practices tailored to meet each individual's unique needs and circumstances. By expanding our definition of self-care, distinguishing it from self-indulgence, ensuring its accessibility, and integrating it into our daily lives, we cultivate a foundation of health and happiness. This foundation supports our personal growth and enhances our capacity to care for others, creating a ripple effect that enriches our communities and beyond.

NOURISHING THE BODY, FEEDING THE SOUL: SELF-CARE FOR PHYSICAL AND MENTAL HEALTH

In the intricate dance of existence, the harmony between physical and mental health plays a pivotal role, acting as the fulcrum upon which our well-being delicately balances. This symbiotic relationship, where the vitality of one feeds into the other, forms the bedrock of a holistic approach to health. It's an acknowledgment that the mind and body are not disparate entities but intertwined aspects of our being, each influencing the other profoundly. Nurturing this connection requires a conscious effort to cater to both, understanding that the nourishment of the body is inextricably linked to the nurturing of the soul.

The act of feeding the body transcends mere sustenance. It is a practice steeped in mindfulness and intention, where each choice of nourishment becomes an act of self-respect. In this context, nutrition emerges not just as a pathway to physical health but as a foundation for self-esteem and overall well-being. Mindful eating, a practice that encourages a deep connection with the food we consume, invites us to experience the textures, flavors, and sensations of our meals, transforming eating from a routine task into a meditative experience. This attentiveness fosters a relationship with food based on nourishment rather than indulgence or restriction, guiding us towards choices that support our health and reflect our care for ourselves. The foods we select, rich in nutrients and vitality, become the building blocks of a body that is cherished and a mind that is nurtured, each meal a step towards an equilibrium where physical well-being and self-esteem flourish in unison.

Parallel to the physical nourishment of the body is the nurturing of the mind, an endeavor that encompasses a spectrum of practices designed to cultivate mental and emotional equilibrium. Central to this pursuit is meditation, a practice that offers a respite from the tumult of daily life through the focusing of the mind and the calming of the spirit. In the silence of meditation, we find clarity, a space where the chatter of the mind recedes, allowing us to connect with a sense of inner peace and grounding. Similarly, journaling serves as a conduit for self-expression, articulating thoughts, emotions, and reflections that might otherwise remain obscured. This practice, akin to a dialogue with oneself, fosters self-awareness and provides a canvas upon which the narrative of our inner lives can unfold. Therapy, too, plays a crucial role in this tapestry of mental health practices, offering professional guidance and support that enables us to navigate the complexities of our emotional landscapes. Together, these practices form a triad of tools at our disposal, each contributing to maintaining a mind as nurtured as the body that houses it.

Integral to the union of physical and mental well-being is the art of attunement to the body's signals. This practice requires an acute awareness of the messages our bodies convey. This attentiveness to bodily cues, whether they manifest as hunger, fatigue, or discomfort, is a form of communication, a dialogue between the mind and the body that informs our self-care choices. Learning to interpret these signals allows us to respond with practices that align with our needs, whether it be restorative sleep, nourishing food, or physical activity. It is a dynamic process that adapts to the changing rhythms of our lives and the evolving needs of our bodies. This responsiveness to the body's language is not just an act of care but a declaration of respect for the intricate vessel that carries us through life.

In this confluence of physical nourishment, mindful practices, and attunement to the body's signals, we find a holistic approach to health that encompasses the totality of our being. It is a recognition that the care of the body cannot be divorced from the nurturing of the mind and that the health of one feeds into the well-being of the other. This interdependence underscores the importance of a balanced approach to self-care, which honors our complex beings and the intricate lives we lead. In nurturing both body and soul, we cultivate a foundation of health and self-esteem that supports us in navigating the challenges and joys of existence, each step taken in mindfulness a stride towards a harmonized and flourishing life.

QUIET TIME: THE ROLE OF SOLITUDE IN SELF-DISCOVERY

In the tapestry of self-care practices, solitude emerges as a nuanced and often misunderstood thread, weaving its way through the fabric of our lives with the potential to profoundly enrich our understanding of one's self. Within the silent embrace of solitude, we find a sanctuary for introspection, a space where the voices that guide, doubt, and define us can be heard with clarity. This is not the solitude born of isolation or loneliness, but a chosen quietude that fosters self-discovery and growth. Here, in the stillness, we meet ourselves unadorned, engaging in a dialogue with our innermost thoughts and feelings, embarking on a journey of self-awareness that illuminates the contours of our being.

The cultivation of solitude as a facet of self-care necessitates a shift in perspective, recognizing its value not as a retreat from the world but as an intentional exploration of the self. In this exploration, practices such as mindfulness techniques and reflective journaling serve as compasses, guiding us through the terrains of our inner landscape. Mindfulness, with its roots anchored in present-moment awareness, teaches us to observe our thoughts and emotions without judgment and sit with them in quiet observance. This practice, whether seated in meditation or woven through the activities of daily living, allows us to disentangle from the constant flow of stimuli to find peace in the pause between thoughts. Similarly, reflective journaling offers a canvas for our inner narrative, where thoughts can be untangled and emotions unpacked. Through writing, we engage in self-discovery, each word a step towards understanding the complexities of our desires, fears, and joys.

Yet, for many, the prospect of solitude stirs a deep-seated discomfort, a fear of what might surface in the quiet. This apprehension is often rooted in misconceptions about solitude, equating it with loneliness or viewing it as time lost from productive pursuits. Overcoming these fears requires a gentle reacquaintance with one's self, a gradual immersion into the quiet that allows us to acclimate to our own company. It begins with short periods of solitude, moments stolen from the day for quiet reflection or simply to be. In these moments, we learn to become comfortable with our presence and appreciate our inner world's richness. As comfort grows, so too does the duration of solitude we seek, each experience building upon the last, fostering a relationship with the self that is both nurturing and enlightening.

The distinction between solitude and loneliness is crucial, for while the former is a chosen state of quiet reflection, the latter is an imposed sense of isolation, a feeling of disconnection from others. Solitude, in its essence, is productive, a state of being that enriches and invigorates the self. Loneliness, conversely, drains and diminishes, leaving feelings of emptiness in its wake. To tread the path of solitude without veering into loneliness requires an anchoring in purpose, an understanding that this quiet time is a gift to one's self, a period of nurturing that strengthens rather than isolates. In balancing solitude with meaningful connections, in weaving quiet time with the threads of community and companionship, we find a harmonious rhythm that honors our need for reflection and connection.

In embracing solitude, we unlock doors to rooms within ourselves previously unexplored, discovering facets of our being that hold the keys to our desires, motivations, and truths. This solitary journey, far from a selfish indulgence, is an act of profound self-care that allows us to return to the world replenished with a deeper understanding of who we are and what we need to thrive. Here, in the stillness, we lay the foundations for a resilient self-esteem informed by an intimate knowledge of our strengths, weaknesses, and innate worth.

THE JOY OF MOVEMENT: EXERCISE AS A PILLAR OF SELF-ESTEEM

In the realm of self-care, incorporating physical activity into our daily routines is a testament to the profound relationship between movement and self-perception. This connection, rooted in the very fibers of our being, offers a pathway to enhanced self-esteem and a more positive body image. The rhythmic contraction and expansion of muscles, the steady rhythm of breath, and the graceful coordination of movement strengthen the body and fortify the mind, weaving a tapestry of well-being that extends far beyond the physical realm.

The transformative power of exercise on self-esteem is palpable, offering a mirror in which we see reflected not our perceived shortcomings, but our strength, resilience, and capacity for growth. This reflection, borne out of the commitment to movement, illuminates the beauty of our physical forms, teaching us to appreciate the functionality and uniqueness of our bodies. Regular engagement in physical activity cultivates a sense of achievement; each step, stroke, or stretch is a building block in the tower of self-worth. As our physical capabilities expand, so does our belief in our competence and value, a correlation supported by numerous studies that highlight the positive impact of exercise on body image and self-esteem.

Pursuing joy in movement is fundamental, transforming exercise from a burdensome obligation to a source of pleasure and fulfillment. The key lies in discovering activities that resonate with our passions and interests, be it the fluidity of dance, the tranquility of yoga, or the exhilaration of running. This alignment of movement with personal joy fosters a more profound engagement, where time spent exercising becomes a celebration of capability rather than a chore. It encourages consistency, as the anticipation of pleasure draws us back to the activity, creating a self-sustaining cycle of physical activity and emotional upliftment.

Beneath the surface of physical benefits lies the profound psychological impact of exercise, a realm where the mind and body converge in a dance of well-being. The act of moving our bodies triggers a cascade of biochemical reactions, releasing endorphins and serotonin, neurotransmitters that act as natural antidotes to stress, anxiety, and depression. This biochemical shift, often referred to as the "runner's high," offers a glimpse into the intricate relationship between physical activity and mental health, where exercise becomes a conduit for emotional regulation and psychological resilience. The repetitive nature of many physical activities, from swimming laps to cycling, induces a meditative state, allowing thoughts to flow freely, untethered from the constraints of worry and stress. This meditative aspect of exercise, coupled with the tangible accomplishment that comes with completing a physical challenge, nurtures a sense of inner peace and confidence radiating through all facets of life.

Starting small offers a gentle entry point for those standing at the threshold of incorporating exercise into their lives. It is an acknowledgment that the journey to physical well-being does not demand grand gestures or monumental efforts but can begin with the simplest of actions. A walk around the block, a brief stretching session, or a few minutes of body-weight exercises at home can serve as the initial steps to a more active lifestyle. This gradual approach, rooted in the understanding that consistency outweighs intensity, allows for the natural integration of movement into daily routines, reducing entry barriers and fostering a sustainable relationship with exercise. It is a process of discovery, where each small step reveals newfound strengths and capabilities, reinforcing the belief in our own efficacy and worth.

As we weave the thread of exercise into the fabric of self-care, the narrative that unfolds is one of transformation and empowerment. In its myriad forms, physical activity stands as a pillar of self-esteem, offering a foundation upon which a positive self-image and a robust sense of self-worth can be built. It is a celebration of the body's capabilities, a journey of discovery that teaches us to find joy in movement, and a practice that nurtures the mind-body connection, contributing to our overall well-being. In this light, exercise emerges not as a mere component of physical health but as a vital element of self-care, a source of strength, confidence, and joy that enriches our lives.

As we close this segment, let us carry forward the understanding that self-care encompasses a diverse spectrum of practices, each contributing to our well-being in unique and meaningful ways. With its capacity to uplift both body and mind, exercise is a testament to the intricate interplay between physical activity and self-esteem. It reminds us that the pursuit of well-being is a multifaceted journey, where the care of the body is inextricably linked to nurturing the soul. In embracing the joy of movement, we step into a broader narrative of self-care that prepares us to explore the rich tapestry of practices that foster our growth, resilience, and happiness. As we transition to the next chapter, let us hold onto the insights gleaned from the pillars of self-care, ready to delve deeper into the journey toward holistic well-being.

BOUNDARIES AND SELF-WORTH

The canvas of life, rich with endless interactions and myriad connections, holds within its frame the delicate art of setting boundaries. Much like the masterful strokes of a painter delineating light from shadow, boundaries distinguish our personal space from the world around us. They serve not merely as barriers but as expressions of our self-worth, a declaration of the respect we demand and the respect we extend to others. In this chapter, we explore the intricate dance of setting boundaries, which, when mastered, fortifies our sense of self and enhances our interactions with the world.

THE ART OF SAYING NO: BOUNDARIES FOR SELF-PRESERVATION

Understanding Boundaries

Boundaries, in their essence, are the invisible lines that define the periphery of our personal space, both physical and emotional. They are the parameters within which we allow others to interact with us, informed by our values, beliefs, and comfort level in various situations. Like the banks of a river that contain and direct its flow, boundaries guide the current of our relationships, ensuring they nourish rather than erode the landscape of our lives. Their significance in fostering healthy interactions cannot be overstated, for boundaries are the bedrock upon which mutual respect and understanding are built.

The Power of "No"

The word 'no' carries within it the power to affirm our boundaries, yet it often weighs heavy on our tongues, burdened by the fear of disappointing others or disrupting the harmony of our relationships. However, saying no is a fundamental right, a verbal embodiment of our boundaries that signals our refusal to compromise our well-being for the sake of others' demands or expectations. It is a complete sentence requiring no justification, embellishment, or apology. When articulated with confidence and clarity, 'no' becomes a shield, protecting the sacred territory of our self-esteem.

Consider the scenario where a friend asks for a favor that stretches beyond your capacity or comfort zone. While difficult, the decision to decline is an exercise in self-respect, a testament to the value you place on your own needs and limits. In this act of refusal, you honor not only your boundaries but also the authenticity of the relationship, offering truth where placation would erode your sense of self.

Practical Steps to Setting Boundaries

Establishing boundaries is a skill that requires introspection, clarity, and assertiveness. Begin by identifying your limits across various dimensions of life—physical, emotional, intellectual, and spiritual. Reflect on past experiences where you felt discomfort or resentment, signals that your boundaries were being tested or crossed.

Next, communicate your boundaries with precision and firmness. This conversation, best approached calmly and directly, involves expressing your needs and expectations clearly, without ambiguity. For instance, informing a colleague that work-related calls after hours are unacceptable sets a clear boundary around your personal time.

Dealing with Boundary Pushers

Despite our best efforts, there will be instances where our boundaries are challenged, either through ignorance or willful disregard. In these moments, reinforcement becomes crucial. Respond to boundary violations consistently and calmly, reiterating your limits without escalation. Should the behavior persist, consider distancing yourself from the situation or relationship, a challenging but sometimes necessary act of self-preservation.

Imagine you've told a persistent acquaintance you're unavailable for late-night conversations, yet the calls continue. A firm, repeated declaration of your boundary and a refusal to engage beyond your stated limits reaffirm your commitment to your well-being.

Visual Element: Boundary Setting Worksheet

A worksheet divided into sections—Identification, Communication, Enforcement—guides the reader through establishing and maintaining boundaries. Each section contains prompts for reflection and action, such as "List instances where you felt your boundaries were disregarded" and "Draft a script for communicating a boundary to a friend."

This chapter, dedicated to the art of saying no and the broader practice of setting boundaries, invites you on a journey of self-discovery and empowerment. By thoughtfully delineating our personal limits, we protect our well-being and cultivate relationships marked by mutual respect and understanding. By mastering the art of boundary setting, we stand firm in our self-worth, navigating the complexities of interaction with grace and strength.

DIGITAL DETOX: SETTING BOUNDARIES WITH TECHNOLOGY

In an era where the digital realm infiltrates almost every aspect of daily existence, the boundary between the virtual and the tangible blurs, leaving our self-esteem vulnerable to the whims of online interactions. The relentless engagement with technology, while offering unparalleled access to information and connectivity, harbors a shadow side—a potential to erode the very foundation of our self-worth. This erosion manifests not in the grand gestures of digital drama but in the quiet moments of comparison, in the silent accumulation of likes and shares that weigh heavily on our perception of one's self. The insidious nature of this impact calls for a deliberate countermeasure, a recalibration of our relationship with digital devices through a digital detox.

The imperative for such a detox stems from a growing body of evidence linking excessive technology use to declining self-esteem. The mechanism of this decline is multifaceted, rooted in the distortion of social comparison, the displacement of real-world interactions, and the constant bombardment of curated realities that skew our perception of normalcy. Each swipe, click, and scroll feeds into a cycle of comparison and dissatisfaction, which, if left unchecked, can diminish our sense of self-worth and contribute to feelings of inadequacy and isolation. Recognizing this dynamic is the first step in reclaiming our digital agency, setting the stage for a detox to restore balance and foster a healthier interaction with technology.

The benefits of periodically disconnecting from our digital devices extend beyond the realm of self-esteem, touching on the very essence of our mental and emotional well-being. A digital detox offers a reprieve from the constant stimulation of the online world, allowing our minds to reset and recharge. This mental respite can improve concentration, reduce stress levels, and create a heightened sense of presence in our immediate surroundings. Emotionally, the space created by a detox can facilitate more profound connections with others, fostering relationships built on the richness of face-to-face interaction rather than the superficiality of digital communication. The quiet that accompanies a detox, devoid of the constant pings and notifications, invites introspection and self-reflection, providing an opportunity to reconnect with our values, desires, and aspirations outside the digital echo chamber.

Crafting a personalized digital detox plan requires thoughtful consideration of our digital habits and their impact on our daily lives. The process begins with an audit of technology use, identifying the platforms and devices that command most of our attention and evaluating their contribution to our well-being. With this insight, we can design a detox plan tailored to our individual needs, setting realistic goals for reduced digital consumption. This might involve designated tech-free hours, particularly during the morning and before bedtime, to mitigate the influence of technology on our sleep and mental state. Alternatively, it could entail the selective unfollowing or muting of social media accounts that trigger feelings of comparison or inadequacy, curating a digital environment that uplifts rather than undermines.

The execution of a digital detox plan, while grounded in personal motivation, benefits from the support of clear strategies and accountability measures. Informing friends and family of our intention to detox can create a support system that encourages adherence to our goals. Replacing digital activities with tangible alternatives—such as reading, exercising, or engaging in hobbies— offers constructive outlets for the time and energy previously devoted to screens. Keeping a journal throughout the detox provides a reflective space to document experiences, challenges, and insights gained from the process, reinforcing the benefits and guiding future detox endeavors.

Maintaining a healthy balance between online and offline life post-detox hinges on integrating mindful technology use into our daily routines. This integration involves the continued practice of tech-free periods, the conscious consumption of digital content, and the cultivation of activities that enrich our lives beyond the screen. Setting intentional boundaries around technology use, such as limiting social media to specific times or purposes, ensures that our engagement remains purposeful rather than habitual. Regularly reassessing our relationship with technology, in light of our evolving needs and priorities, enables us to adapt our digital boundaries, ensuring they continue to serve our well-being and self-esteem.

In navigating the complex landscape of technology and self-worth, the deliberate practice of setting boundaries through a digital detox emerges as a powerful tool for self-preservation. It is an acknowledgment of the profound impact of the digital realm on our perception of self and a commitment to fostering a healthier, more balanced interaction with technology. Through this practice, we safeguard our self-esteem and reclaim the richness of a life lived with intentionality and presence, undiminished by the digital world.

EMOTIONAL BOUNDARIES: PROTECTING YOUR HEART

In the labyrinth of human relationships, emotional boundaries serve as the invisible yet palpable force fields that safeguard our inner sanctum from external intrusions. These subtle yet potent boundaries delineate the perimeters within which our emotional exchanges occur, ensuring that the flux of empathy, care, and understanding flows freely yet remains contained, preventing the seepage of negativity or the inundation of our emotional reserves. Cultivating these boundaries is an act of self-preservation, a testament to our reverence for our emotional well-being. Within this context, we turn our attention to the identification of emotional drainers, the establishment of emotional boundaries, the nurturing of our emotional health, and the adept navigation through the storms of emotional challenges.

Identifying Emotional Drainers

The landscape of our lives is dotted with many interactions, each carrying the potential to enrich or deplete our emotional energy. Emotional drainers, often cloaked in the guise of routine exchanges or entrenched relationships, possess the insidious ability to sap our vitality, leaving a residue of fatigue, discontent, or disillusionment. Recognizing these drainers necessitates a keen attunement to our emotional responses, an awareness that whispers caution when our spirits wane in the presence of certain individuals or situations. It is the tightening in our chest during a conversation that veers into criticism, the lethargy that follows interactions fraught with pessimism, or the shadow of inadequacy that lingers after encounters with those who belittle or negate.

This recognition, though unsettling, serves as the first beacon toward the reclamation of our emotional equilibrium.

Setting Emotional Boundaries

The demarcation of emotional boundaries is akin to the drawing of a map that charts the territories where our emotional well-being reigns supreme. This process begins with articulating our emotional needs and limits, a declaration of the environments, interactions, and behaviors we find conducive to our well-being versus those we deem detrimental. The communication of these boundaries, imbued with the clarity and conviction of our self-worth, is essential. It might manifest in the gentle yet firm refusal to engage in gossip, the explicit request for respect in discourse, or the delineation of topics that we find emotionally taxing. This articulation, while potentially fraught with the risk of dissent or conflict, stands as a bulwark against the encroachment of our emotional peace.

Self-Care for Emotional Health

The tapestry of self-care, rich with threads of physical and intellectual practices, reserves a golden strand dedicated to emotional health within its weave. This strand encompasses a spectrum of practices, each designed to fortify our emotional resilience and nurture the garden of our feelings. Mindfulness, with its roots in the present and its branches reaching toward acceptance, offers solace, allowing us to observe our emotions without entanglement, acknowledging their presence without succumbing to their sway. The practice of gratitude, a beacon in the tumult of distress, shifts the lens through which we view our lives, highlighting the abundance that resides alongside adversity. Engaging in activities that resonate with our passions—be it art, music, or nature—acts as a balm, a salve that soothes the frayed edges of our emotions, reminding us of the beauty and expansiveness of our experience. These practices, individually tailored and collectively embraced, weave a protective cocoon around our emotional well-being, insulating us from the vicissitudes of life.

Navigating Emotional Challenges

The voyage through the seas of life, replete with its storms and doldrums, tests the integrity of our emotional boundaries. Navigating these challenges, whether they arise from personal loss, conflict, or the inherent complexities of human relationships, demands a compass calibrated by self-awareness and resilience. It requires the ability to anchor ourselves amid turbulence, to recognize the transient nature of our emotions, and to seek solace in the knowledge that we possess the tools to weather the storm. This navigation is facilitated by a network of support, a constellation of trusted individuals whose wisdom, empathy, and perspective can illuminate the path through the darkness. It is further aided by the practice of self-compassion, a gentle acknowledgment of our vulnerability and strength, allowing us to extend the same kindness to ourselves that we would to a beloved friend. Through these means, we traverse the challenges, emerging not unscathed but fortified, our emotional boundaries intact and our hearts still open to the vastness of our human experience.

WORKPLACE BOUNDARIES: NAVIGATING PROFESSIONAL RELATIONSHIPS

The intricate tapestry of professional interactions demarcates the spheres of personal and professional life, a testament to the complexity of human relationships within the workplace. This delineation, essential for maintaining self-esteem and a harmonious work-life balance, requires a nuanced understanding and strategic navigation to ensure that one preserves the sanctity of one's personal space even as one engages in the collaborative and often competitive arena of professional endeavors.

The separation of professional and personal realms is not merely a logistical arrangement but a psychological imperative. It safeguards the individual's sense of self, enabling a clear distinction between roles assumed in professional settings and the authenticity of personal identity. This boundary prevents the encroachment of work-related stress into the sanctuary of personal life, ensuring that the challenges and triumphs of the professional world do not overshadow the individual's holistic self-perception. Strategies to uphold this separation include setting clear expectations regarding availability, delineating physical spaces dedicated to work, and fostering hobbies and relationships outside the professional sphere, each acting as a bulwark against the potential erosion of self-esteem by work demands.

Assertiveness in the workplace, characterized by the capacity to communicate one's needs and opinions with confidence and respect, emerges as a pivotal skill in establishing professional boundaries. It involves articulating thoughts and expectations with clarity and advocating for one's interests without infringing on the rights and dignity of others. This assertive communication, far from an aggressive assertion of dominance, is a balanced expression of self-respect and mutual respect, an acknowledgment of one's worth and the worth of colleagues. Techniques to cultivate assertiveness include practicing clear and concise communication, preparing for potential conversations in advance, and employing assertive body language, each contributing to an atmosphere where boundaries are respected and professionalism is maintained.

The phenomenon of overwork and the resultant stress, pervasive in contemporary professional landscapes, underscores the imperative for setting boundaries around work hours and responsibilities. The glorification of busyness, often mistaken for dedication or ambition, can lead to burnout, diminishing professional efficacy and personal well-being. Establishing limits on work hours, learning to delegate tasks, and prioritizing responsibilities based on urgency and importance become acts of self-care. They signal a commitment to one's health and a recognition that productivity is not measured by hours spent but by the quality of work and the worker's well-being. This approach emphasizes balance, respects the individual's capacity, and fosters a sustainable engagement with work.

Cultivating supportive professional networks and communities bound by shared goals and mutual respect plays a crucial role in navigating the complexities of workplace relationships. These networks, formed through genuine connections and nurtured by shared experiences, offer a reservoir of resources, advice, and support. Within these communities, the exchange of knowledge flourishes, mentorship relationships blossom, and a sense of belonging is fostered, all contributing to a positive work environment. The act of building these networks, intentional and rooted in authenticity, requires openness, a willingness to connect, and a commitment to contributing to the collective well-being of the community.

In the realm of professional interactions, the art of boundary setting emerges as a critical skill, a dynamic interplay between the assertion of self and the cultivation of healthy, supportive relationships. It is a delicate balance, requiring constant attention and adjustment, informed by self-awareness and a deep respect for the individuality and aspirations of oneself and others. Individuals navigate the multifaceted landscape of workplace relationships through the strategic delineation of personal and professional spheres, the practice of assertive communication, the mindful management of work-related stress, and the intentional building of supportive networks. These practices, collectively embraced, enhance self-esteem and work-life balance and contribute to a culture of respect, empathy, and mutual support within the professional arena.

In closing, the journey through the intricacies of setting boundaries in personal, digital, emotional, and professional contexts reveals a common thread—the profound impact of these boundaries on our self-esteem, relationships, and overall quality of life. By embracing the principles of assertiveness, mindfulness, and self-respect, we fortify our sense of self and cultivate environments where growth, well-being, and mutual respect flourish. As we transition to the next chapter, let us carry forward the insights gained, ready to explore new horizons in our continuous quest for self-discovery, empowerment, and fulfillment.

CONQUERING THE INNER CRITIC

In the quiet recesses of our minds, a voice whispers, casting shadows of doubt and criticism over our accomplishments and aspirations. This voice, known as the inner critic, wields a subtle yet profound influence on our self-esteem, shaping our perceptions of ourselves and our capabilities. Far from the supportive companion we deserve, this critic often emerges as our most persistent detractor, a presence that, if left unchecked, can erode the very foundations of our self-worth.

THE INNER CRITIC: UNDERSTANDING ITS ORIGINS

Roots of the Critic

The psychological origins of the inner critic can be traced back to early life experiences and societal influences. Like a seed planted in the fertile soil of our psyche, the inner critic grows from the messages we receive in childhood, whether from parents, teachers, or peers. These messages, imbued with expectations and judgments, weave into the fabric of our self-perception, shaping the voice that later critiques our every move. With its relentless standards and norms, society further nourishes this critic, bombarding us with ideals of success, beauty, and behavior that become internal benchmarks against which we measure ourselves.

Consider the experience of standing in front of a room, about to deliver a presentation. The inner critic might whisper doubts about your preparation, question your expertise, or predict the audience's disapproval. This scenario underscores the critic's power to influence our confidence and actions, often based on deep-seated beliefs formed in our earlier years.

Recognizing the Voice

Identifying when the inner critic speaks is the first step toward mitigating its impact. This voice often masquerades as our own thoughts, making it challenging to distinguish. Yet, its patterns are recognizable—absolute statements that brook no argument, such as "You always fail" or "You'll never be good enough." These messages, steeped in negativity and devoid of compassion, are the critic's trademarks, starkly contrasting the supportive, nuanced thoughts we might otherwise nurture.

Impact on Self-Worth

The unchecked negative self-talk propagated by the inner critic can significantly erode self-esteem and hinder personal growth. By constantly undermining our achievements and magnifying our faults, the critic skews our self-image, leading us to underestimate our worth and potential. The consequences of this erosion manifest in various aspects of life, from professional stagnation to strained relationships, as we navigate the world through a lens colored by doubt and self-criticism.

Shifting Perspective

Viewing the inner critic as a misguided protector rather than an inherent adversary offers a pathway to a more compassionate self-dialogue. This perspective acknowledges the critic's origins in protective mechanisms—efforts to shield us from failure or rejection by setting high standards or discouraging risk. By understanding this intent, we can begin negotiating with the critic, acknowledging its concerns while challenging its negative assertions. This shift paves the way for a dialogue rooted in self-compassion, where kindness and understanding temper the critic's harshness.

Visual Element: Recognizing the Inner Critic Worksheet

A worksheet provides a structured approach to identifying and addressing the inner critic. Sections prompt reflection on recent self-criticism, encouraging users to record the critic's messages, the emotions they elicited, and the situations that triggered them. Further prompts guide the re-evaluation of these messages from a perspective of compassion and realism, encouraging a balanced view of oneself.

This exploration into the depths of the inner critic illuminates its profound impact on our self-esteem and personal growth. By understanding its origins, recognizing its voice, and learning to shift our perspective, we can transform our self-dialogue from criticism to compassion. This transformation marks a crucial step toward silencing the doubts and embracing a self-view marked by kindness, understanding, and unwavering self-worth.

FLIPPING THE SCRIPT: FROM CRITICISM TO COMPASSION

Amidst the din of self-criticism, a whisper of self-compassion emerges, a tender yet potent force capable of transforming the harsh narratives we often hold about ourselves. This transformation begins with recognizing self-compassion not merely as an antidote to the inner critic but as a fundamental shift in how we engage with ourselves at moments of perceived failure or inadequacy. Self-compassion invites us to extend the same grace, understanding, and kindness to ourselves that we would naturally offer to a dear friend in distress. It's an acknowledgment of our shared humanity, an acceptance of imperfection as a universal trait rather than a personal flaw.

Incorporating mindfulness practices is a foundational step in detaching from and observing negative self-talk without the cloud of judgment. Mindfulness, the practice of anchoring oneself in the present moment with a stance of open curiosity, allows us to notice our inner dialogue without becoming trapped by it. Through mindfulness, we observe our thoughts as if they were leaves floating down a stream — noticeable, but not defining. This detachment provides the space to question the validity of the inner critic's assertions and to see them as habitual patterns of thought rather than immutable truths. Mindfulness meditation, focused breathing exercises, and mindful walking are practical tools that facilitate this shift in perspective; each practice is a thread in the fabric of a compassionate relationship with oneself.

Cultivating kindness towards oneself, particularly in moments of struggle or self-doubt, reinforces the foundation of self-compassion. It's an active process that involves consciously replacing self-critical thoughts with messages of support and encouragement. This might manifest as a mental pause when the inner critic speaks, followed by a deliberate choice to offer oneself words of kindness and understanding. For instance, upon recognizing a thought pattern that underscores inadequacy, one might gently remind oneself, "You're doing the best you can with what you have right now." Such affirmations are not mere platitudes but powerful acts of self-compassion that affirm our worth and resilience.

Building a compassionate inner voice is the most transformative aspect of this journey. It involves nurturing an internal dialogue that supports and encourages rather than condemns. This new voice acknowledges our efforts, forgives our mistakes, and celebrates our progress, however small. Developing this voice can begin with writing letters to oneself, a method that externalizes self-compassion and makes it tangible. In moments of self-doubt or criticism, writing a letter from the perspective of a compassionate friend allows us to externalize the kindness we struggle to afford ourselves. Over time, these letters become a reservoir of compassion we can draw upon, gradually internalizing this nurturing voice until it becomes a natural part of our internal dialogue.

The shift from self-criticism to self-compassion is neither swift nor straightforward. It's a gradual process that requires patience, practice, and a steadfast commitment to treating oneself with the same kindness one would extend to others. It's a journey marked by moments of insight and backslides, each step forward a testament to our capacity for growth and change. Through the practices of mindfulness, the deliberate cultivation of kindness, and the nurturing of a compassionate inner voice, we rewrite the script of our self-dialogue. This new narrative, steeped in self-compassion, becomes a wellspring from which self-esteem and resilience flow, a testament to our inherent worth and the transformative power of kindness turned inward.

THE POWER OF POSITIVE AFFIRMATIONS: REWIRING YOUR BRAIN

Amidst the din of everyday life, where self-doubt and criticism often find fertile ground, the concept of positive affirmations stands as a beacon of transformative potential. Rooted in the intricate workings of the mind, these affirmations are not mere collections of words but potent tools capable of reshaping the neural pathways that govern our thoughts, emotions, and, ultimately, our self-esteem. The science underlying this phenomenon, known as neuroplasticity, reveals the brain's remarkable ability to reorganize itself by forming new neural connections throughout life. This capacity for change provides the foundation upon which the practice of affirmations builds, offering a pathway to counteract negative self-talk and foster a deeply ingrained sense of self-worth.

Engaging in the practice of affirmations activates specific regions within the brain, including those associated with self-processing and valuation. When we affirm our values, capabilities, or positive attributes, we stimulate these areas, reinforcing our sense of self and enhancing our self-esteem. Over time, with consistent practice, this stimulation strengthens the neural pathways that support positive thinking, making them more predominant. It's akin to carving a river through stone; the repeated flow of affirming thoughts gradually reshapes the landscape of our mind, making positive self-perception not just a visitor but a permanent resident within our psyche.

The crafting of personal affirmations is an art that requires both introspection and precision. Begin by identifying areas of life where self-esteem feels most vulnerable—perhaps it's in professional endeavors, personal relationships, or one's relationship with oneself. Within these areas, pinpoint specific beliefs or criticisms that frequently surface. The next step is constructing affirmations that directly counter these negative beliefs, ensuring they are phrased in the present tense, imbued with positivity, and stated as facts. For instance, if the belief is "I am not skilled enough," an effective affirmation could be, "I possess unique talents and skills that I bring to everything I do."

Integrating these affirmations into the fabric of daily life maximizes their impact, transforming them from abstract concepts into tangible truths. This integration can begin with reciting affirmations during moments of quiet reflection, such as upon waking or before sleep when the mind is most receptive. Writing affirmations in a journal or on sticky notes placed in visible locations serves as constant reminders of their truth. Additionally, incorporating affirmations into meditation or mindfulness routines can deepen their resonance, allowing the words to permeate beyond the surface level of consciousness and anchor deeply within the psyche.

Anticipating and addressing skepticism around the efficacy of affirmations is crucial, as doubts can undermine their potential benefits. Skepticism often stems from misunderstanding affirmations as magical thinking or underestimating the brain's capacity for change. Counteracting this skepticism involves examining the evidence supporting neuroplasticity and the documented effects of positive self-talk on mental health and self-esteem. Studies have shown that individuals who engage in positive affirmations exhibit increased activity in neural pathways associated with self-value and future orientation. Furthermore, affirmations have been linked to reduced stress, improved problem-solving under pressure, and greater well-being. Presenting this body of evidence, coupled with personal testimonials or case studies, offers a compelling argument for the power of affirmations to foster profound and lasting changes in self-perception and self-esteem.

In this exploration of positive affirmations, we uncover their potential not only as antidotes to the inner critic but as foundational tools for rewiring the brain towards a state of enhanced self-esteem and well-being. Through the deliberate crafting and integration of affirmations into our daily lives, we engage in an act of self-transformation, harnessing the science of neuroplasticity to cultivate a mind that supports and uplifts, propelling us toward our fullest potential.

SILENCING THE DOUBT: PRACTICAL EXERCISES FOR OVERCOMING SELF-CRITICISM

In the realm of personal growth, the journey toward silencing self-doubt requires an arsenal of tools designed to unearth and transform the deeply ingrained patterns of negative self-talk. This transformative process begins with journaling for self-discovery, a practice that illuminates the hidden corridors of our psyche and empowers us to rewrite the narratives that bind us.

Journaling for Self-Discovery presents itself as a reflective mirror, one that reveals the multifaceted aspects of our internal dialogue. By putting pen to paper, we engage in a dialogue with our deeper selves, uncovering the layers of beliefs and assumptions that shape our self-perception. This practice involves structured prompts that guide us to confront our inner critic head-on, questioning its basis and validity. For instance, journaling entries might focus on instances of self-doubt, encouraging a deep dive into their origins and the evidence that supports or contradicts these beliefs. This written exploration serves as a catalyst for cognitive restructuring, challenging us to replace self-critical thoughts with ones rooted in compassion and truth.

Visualization Techniques further augment this process by harnessing the mind's ability to construct and inhabit positive realities. This method involves creating vivid mental imagery that embodies our desired state of self-acceptance and confidence. By regularly engaging in visualization exercises, such as imagining oneself delivering a successful presentation or navigating a challenging scenario with grace, we begin to shift our self-perception. These mental rehearsals not only prepare us for real-world encounters but also embed a sense of capability and resilience within our psyche, gradually diminishing the space occupied by self-doubt.

Role-Playing Scenarios offer a dynamic approach to confronting and disarming the inner critic. This exercise entails the enactment of conversations or situations where self-criticism typically arises, allowing for the practice of assertive responses to self-doubt. Whether conducted alone in front of a mirror or with a trusted confidant, role-playing facilitates a real-time exploration of alternative narratives, empowering us to vocalize self-affirming truths in place of critical judgments. This active engagement with our inner dialogue fosters a readiness to counteract negative self-talk as it arises, reinforcing a stance of self-support and advocacy.

The foundation of these practices rests on the **Creation of a Support System**, a crucial element that nurtures and sustains our efforts to silence self-doubt. This system, woven from the threads of friendships, mentorships, and communities, offers a reservoir of encouragement, perspective, and validation. By surrounding ourselves with individuals who echo our commitment to positive self-talk and bolster our self-esteem, we fortify our defenses against the inner critic. This supportive network acts as a mirror, reflecting back our strength, worth, and potential, often obscured by the veil of self-criticism. Regular engagement with this system, whether through shared exercises, open discussions about vulnerabilities, or celebrating personal victories, cultivates an environment where self-esteem thrives, nurtured by collective affirmation and understanding.

In navigating the path toward muting the discordant notes of self-doubt, these exercises—journaling for self-discovery, visualization techniques, role-playing scenarios, and cultivating a support system—serve as guideposts. Each tool, unique in its approach, contributes to the overarching goal of transforming our internal dialogue from one of criticism to one of compassion. This transformation, though gradual, is profound, marking a shift in how we perceive and engage with ourselves and the world around us.

As we draw this exploration to a close, the essence of our endeavor comes into focus. It is a commitment not merely to silence self-doubt but to foster a relationship with ourselves that is grounded in kindness, understanding, and unwavering support. Through the practices outlined, we equip ourselves with the means to challenge and reshape the narratives that have long confined us, stepping into a space where our self-esteem is no longer tethered to the whims of the inner critic. This journey, marked by introspection, resilience, and growth, paves the way for a future where our self-worth is defined not by external validation or internal criticism but by the intrinsic value we recognize within ourselves. In this recognition lies the power to transform, to transcend the doubts that once held sway, and to embrace a vision of ourselves that is radiant with confidence and self-acceptance.

FACING FEAR AND FLOURISHING

A tightrope walker, suspended high above the ground, moves with a balance born of practice, every step a defiance of the yawning void below. This image, stark and visceral, mirrors the precipice we find ourselves on when confronted with the fear of failure. It's a moment teetering between the potential for triumph and the risk of a fall, a scenario where the mind's chorus of doubts often drowns out the heart's quiet whispers of courage. In this chapter, we dissect the anatomy of this fear, its roots, and its relentless grip on our self-esteem, and we chart a path through its shadows toward resilience and growth.

THE FEAR OF FALLING: OVERCOMING THE FEAR OF FAILURE

Understanding Fear of Failure

At its core, the fear of failure is a primal response wired deep within our psyche, serving as a cautionary alarm against potential threats to our well-being or social standing. Psychologists point to this fear as a complex interplay of past experiences, learned behaviors, and societal pressures, a concoction that often brews a potent barrier to personal growth. This fear whispers tales of judgment and disappointment, casting long shadows on our aspirations and coloring our choices with hesitation. It's a ubiquitous experience, from a student hesitating to raise a hand in class to an entrepreneur pausing at the brink of a venture, each instance a testament to its pervasive influence.

Reframing Failure

The reframing of failure from an endpoint to a waypoint in the journey of learning marks a pivotal shift in perspective. A study in the "Journal of Personality and Social Psychology" illuminates this approach, revealing that individuals who view failure as a stepping stone rather than a stumbling block are more resilient and adaptive in the face of challenges. This reframe involves a conscious shift in language and thought patterns, transforming "I failed" into "I learned." It's about viewing each misstep not as a mark of defeat but as a vital insight, an instrumental guidepost on mastery. The story of Thomas Edison's myriad attempts before successfully inventing the light bulb serves as a compelling narrative of this mindset, a reminder that brilliance often emerges from the crucible of repeated failure.

Overcoming Perfectionism

Perfectionism, the relentless pursuit of flawlessness, often lies at the heart of the fear of failure, its roots entangling our self-esteem. While seemingly noble, this pursuit shackles us to an unattainable standard, each imperfection a perceived dent in our self-worth. Breaking free from this cycle requires an acknowledgment of perfectionism's paralyzing effect and a deliberate embrace of imperfection. Strategies for this embrace include setting realistic goals, celebrating progress regardless of perfection, and practicing self-compassion. It's about recognizing that the beauty of our endeavors lies not in their faultlessness but in the growth, learning, and resilience they foster.

Building Resilience

Resilience, the ability to bounce back from setbacks, emerges as our bulwark against the fear of failure. This quality does not negate the presence of fear but offers a way to navigate through it. Building resilience involves cultivating a support system, engaging in self-care practices, and adopting a growth mindset. It's about forging a resilience toolkit: mindfulness practices that ground us in the present, affirmations that bolster our self-belief, and a network of support that reminds us of our strength and capability. This toolkit, personalized and honed over time, becomes our lifeline, a source of strength that allows us to face fear with courage and grace.

Visual Element: Chart of Resilience-Building Strategies

A detailed chart categorizes and outlines strategies for enhancing resilience. This visual guide is divided into sections—Mindfulness, Support Systems, Self-Care, and Growth Mindset—each offering practical, actionable steps. For instance, under Mindfulness, the chart suggests daily meditation and breathing exercises; under Support Systems, it recommends seeking mentors and engaging in community groups. This chart serves as a roadmap, guiding readers in assembling their personalized resilience toolkit.

Reflection Section: Journaling Prompts on Fear and Failure

A series of guided journaling prompts encourage deep reflection on personal experiences with fear and failure. Questions like "What is your earliest memory of fearing failure?" and "How has perfectionism held you back?" invite introspection, allowing readers to uncover and examine the roots of their fears. These prompts facilitate self-discovery and foster a shift in perspective, encouraging a more compassionate and constructive engagement with failure.

Confronting the fear of failure requires a delicate dance involving balance, courage, and a deep-rooted belief in our capacity for growth. This chapter, a map through the terrain of fear, offers tools, strategies, and insights to navigate this landscape. It's a guide for those standing on the precipice, ready to step forward, where facing fear becomes a challenge to overcome and an opportunity to flourish.

EMBRACING IMPERFECTION: THE BEAUTY OF BEING FLAWED

In a culture that often peddles the myth of perfection, the quest for flawless existence becomes a Sisyphean task, constantly eluding grasp, perpetuating cycles of dissatisfaction and self-reproach. This myth, deeply entrenched in societal narratives and amplified by curated social media feeds, insists on an unattainable standard and is fundamentally at odds with the essence of human experience. Imperfection, with its inherent messiness and unpredictability, constitutes the very fabric of our individuality, a tapestry of quirks, idiosyncrasies, and flaws that render each of us uniquely fascinating. Recognizing this truth initiates a radical shift, a liberation from the confines of unachievable standards, opening avenues to embrace and celebrate the nuanced complexities that define us.

The cultivation of self-acceptance emerges as a pivotal practice in this embrace, a deliberate process of acknowledging and valuing one's inherent worth independent of achievements, appearances, or the approval of others. This practice begins with cultivating mindfulness, an attunement to the present moment that encourages observing thoughts and feelings without judgment. Through mindfulness, moments of self-criticism are met with curiosity and compassion, creating space to gently challenge and reframe negative perceptions of oneself. Additionally, journaling serves as a reflective tool to document and explore one's thoughts, feelings, and reactions. Through written expression, one can trace patterns of self-criticism, uncovering their roots and gradually shifting towards narratives of self-acceptance and kindness.

Vulnerability, often perceived as a weakness, reveals itself to be a reservoir of strength and authenticity in the context of human connections. In the moments when we lay bare our fears, doubts, and imperfections, we invite genuine intimacy, fostering relationships grounded in mutual understanding and acceptance. This openness acts as a bridge, a conduit for empathy and connection, dissolving the facades that keep us isolated in our struggles. Embracing vulnerability requires courage and a willingness to navigate the discomfort of exposure with the conviction that the authenticity of our connections far outweighs the fear of judgment. In the shared spaces of our imperfections, we find common ground, a collective humanity that binds us in our shared experiences and struggles.

The ability to laugh at oneself and find humor in our missteps and imperfections is a powerful antidote to the weight of self-criticism. This lightness, a playful acknowledgment of our fallibility, diffuses the gravity of our flaws, framing them as facets of our humanity rather than deficits. Laughter, in its spontaneity and joy, reconnects us with the immediacy of the present, a reminder that perfection is not a prerequisite for happiness or worth. By cultivating a sense of humor about our imperfections, we permit ourselves to experience joy and self-compassion amidst the messiness of life. This approach alleviates the emotional burden of striving for an unattainable ideal and enhances our resilience, enabling us to navigate life's challenges with grace and levity.

In navigating the landscape of imperfection, we encounter the freedom of self-acceptance and the beauty of a life lived in authenticity. This journey, marked by the deliberate practices of mindfulness, journaling, vulnerability, and humor, invites a reevaluation of the standards by which we measure our worth. It challenges the societal myth of perfection, advocating instead for celebrating the unique mosaic of traits and experiences that make us who we are. In this embrace of imperfection, we find the courage to be ourselves and the grace to accept and love ourselves, flaws and all.

LESSONS IN FAILURE: STORIES OF RESILIENCE

In the vast expanse of human experience, where triumphs and setbacks paint the canvas of our lives in broad strokes of emotion and learning, the narratives of individuals who have encountered failure only to rise, Phoenix-like, from the ashes, serve as beacons of hope and fortitude. These tales, each unique in their contours yet universal in their themes of persistence and resilience, illuminate the path for those grappling with the specter of failure, offering not just solace but a blueprint for transformation.

Consider the arc of an athlete, once heralded as a prodigy, who encounters a string of defeats that cast a pall over a promising career. The public's adulation turns to scrutiny, and self-doubt creeps in, eroding the foundation of confidence that once seemed unshakable. Yet, within this crucible of failure, a metamorphosis occurs. Through introspection and relentless determination, the athlete redefines the essence of success, not as an accumulation of victories but as an unwavering commitment to excellence and growth. Once a chore, training sessions transform into sanctuaries of meditation and improvement, each drop of sweat a testament to the athlete's resilience. When it arrives, the comeback is not just a return to form but a renaissance of spirit, a narrative that underscores the profound strength inherent in embracing and transcending failure.

The framework for dissecting these setbacks, to cull wisdom from the residue of disappointment, hinges on a meticulous process of analysis—a deliberate deconstruction of events to identify both missteps and missed opportunities. This analytical lens, applied with the precision of a scholar and the empathy of a confidant, encourages a dispassionate examination of the factors contributing to failure. Questions serve as the scalpels in this intellectual surgery, probing the depth of our decisions, strategies, and reactions. What alternative paths could have been taken? Where did judgment falter, and why? How did emotions, whether hubris or fear, color our choices? This inquiry, rigorous yet imbued with kindness, allows for extracting actionable insights, transforming failure from a shadowy specter into a luminous guidepost.

A remarkable alchemy occurs in altering our vantage point on failure and viewing it through the prism of opportunity rather than the lens of defeat. In this light, failure morphs into a catalyst for growth, a force that propels us forward with renewed vigor and vision. It becomes a motivator, its sting tempered by the recognition of its value in the crucible of character building. This shift in perspective, subtle yet profound, recasts setbacks as milestones in self-improvement, imbuing them with a sense of purpose and potential. It is a reorientation that champions the process over the outcome, acknowledging that the journey, with its array of experiences and emotions, holds intrinsic worth beyond the tally of successes and failures.

Regardless of the outcome, celebrating progress emerges as a vital practice in cultivating a healthy relationship with failure. It affirms effort and intent, recognizing that merit resides not solely in achieving goals but in the courage to pursue them. This practice involves setting incremental milestones, each achievement a cause for acknowledgment and joy. It's a ritual that fosters an environment where failure is not a deterrent but a part of the learning process, a step in the continuum of growth. In this space, effort is lauded, progress is honored, and setbacks are viewed as precursors to insight, each contributing to the tapestry of our evolving selves.

In the narratives of resilience that pepper the landscape of human endeavor, from the athlete's journey of redemption to the entrepreneur's tale of perseverance amid adversity, the lessons of failure emerge as pivotal chapters in the story of success. These lessons, mined from the depths of disappointment and analyzed with a keen eye for learning, underscore the transformative power of perspective. They remind us that failure, when approached with introspection, courage, and an unwavering commitment to growth, becomes not just an inevitable waypoint but a powerful instrument of self-discovery and empowerment. In this recognition lies the key to navigating the complexities of failure, transforming it from an endpoint into a launchpad for resilience, innovation, and unparalleled achievement.

RISK-TAKING AND GROWTH: LEAVING THE COMFORT ZONE

In the vast expanse of personal evolution, the willingness to engage with uncertainty is a pivotal axis upon which growth and self-esteem pivot. This engagement, often encapsulated in the act of taking calculated risks, propels us into previously uncharted realms of experience and learning. Here, at the precipice of the familiar and the unknown, the seeds of transformation find fertile ground, germinating into forms of self-assurance and capability that reshape our understanding of what is possible.

The essence of growth through risk-taking lies not in reckless abandon but in the judicious appraisal of potential actions against the backdrop of one's values and aspirations. This appraisal involves a meticulous analysis, weighing the benefits and consequences of stepping beyond the known confines of comfort. The strategies for such assessments intertwine intuition with logic, creating a balanced approach to decision-making. One might, for instance, employ decision trees or pros-and-cons lists as tools to visually map out the potential outcomes of risk, grounding abstract considerations in concrete terms. While methodical, this process also leaves room for the gut feelings that often guide us toward decisions that resonate with our core selves, even without tangible evidence.

Navigating the trepidation that accompanies ventures into the unknown demands a repertoire of techniques designed to modulate fear, transforming it from a barrier to a beacon. This modulation begins with acknowledging fear as a natural response, a protective mechanism wired into our biology. However, its presence does not dictate our actions. Mindfulness and breathing exercises can serve as anchors, bringing us back to a state of calm presence where fear does not overwhelm us. Visualization, too, plays a critical role, allowing us to rehearse scenarios mentally, reducing the unknowns that often fuel fear. By visualizing successful outcomes or managing challenges adeptly, we reinforce our belief in our ability to navigate risks effectively.

The initiation into risk-taking often starts with small, manageable steps, a gentle but deliberate expansion of the boundaries of our comfort zone. These initial forays into the realm of risk serve a dual purpose: they build the muscles of courage and resilience while providing tangible evidence of our capacity to face uncertainty. It might begin with voicing an unpopular opinion in a meeting, signing up for a class in an unfamiliar subject, or even changing a habitual routine. Though seemingly inconsequential, each act lays a brick in the foundation of our confidence, creating a momentum that propels us toward larger, more significant changes. It's a cumulative process, where each risk, regardless of its outcome, contributes to a tapestry of experiences that enrich our understanding of ourselves and our potential.

As we tread the path of risk-taking, we find that the contours of our comfort zone expand, reshaped by our ventures into the unknown. This expansion is not merely a byproduct of action but a testament to the transformation within, a reflection of self-esteem enhanced by the knowledge that we possess the strength to face uncertainty and emerge not diminished but enriched. In this enrichment, the true value of risk-taking lies not in the specific outcomes of each venture but in the cumulative effect on our perception of ourselves and our place in the world.

In embracing the uncertainty that accompanies risk, we unlock doors to the potential that resides just beyond the threshold of our comfort zones. This journey, marked by the careful assessment of risks, the management of fear, and the strategic embrace of small challenges, reveals a landscape rich with opportunity and growth. It teaches us that within the heart of risk lies the seed of possibility, which, when nurtured by action and reflection, blossoms into a self-assuredness that transcends the boundaries of what we once deemed possible.

As we draw this exploration to a close, we find ourselves standing at the edge of comprehension, gazing out at a horizon where risk and growth are inextricably linked. The steps we take, informed by thoughtful assessment and fueled by a willingness to navigate fear, pave the way for transformations that redefine our understanding of ourselves and our capabilities. In this journey, each challenge faced, and each boundary crossed, contributes to a narrative of self-discovery and empowerment. In this narrative, stepping out of our comfort zones becomes a venture into the unknown and a passage to a more profound, more resilient version of ourselves. As we move forward, let us carry the insights and strategies gleaned from this chapter, ready to embrace the risks that herald our evolution and the growth that awaits on the other side of fear.

RISE AND SHINE: A WOMAN'S BLUEPRINT FOR HIGH SELF-ESTEEM

Make a Difference with Your Review
Unlock the Power of High Self-Esteem

Helping one person might not change the whole world, but it could change the world for one person.

— ANONYMOUS

Did you know that people who help others without expecting anything in return tend to feel happier, more fulfilled, and even find more success in their lives? Well, if there's a chance for us to experience that together, you bet we're going to take it!

Here's something to ponder...

Would you be willing to lend a hand to someone you've never met, even if you knew you wouldn't get a 'thank you'?

Imagine this person. They might remind you of yourself at another time in your life. Perhaps less confident, eager to grow, and looking for guidance but not sure where to find it.

Our goal is to share the secrets of high self-esteem with everyone. Everything I do is aimed at this goal. But to truly reach everyone, we need a little help from friends like you.

The truth is, most people do judge a book by its cover—and its reviews. So, I'm reaching out to ask for a favor on behalf of someone struggling with self-esteem, whom you've never met:

Could you take a moment to leave a review for this book?

This simple act doesn't cost a thing and takes less than a minute, but it could forever change the life of someone just like you. Your review might help:

...one more person feel confident in their own skin. ...one more individual chase their dreams with conviction. ...one more soul to find peace and happiness within. ...one more life to be filled with joy and self-love. ...one more story of transformation and triumph.

To share a bit of joy and truly make a difference, all you need to do is leave a review. It's quick and easy:

Simply scan the QR code below to share your thoughts:

If the thought of helping someone in this way makes you smile, then you're definitely my kind of person. Welcome to the club. You're part of our family now.

I can't wait to help you build higher self-esteem and find even more joy and fulfillment in your life. You're going to love the insights and strategies waiting for you in the pages ahead.

Thank you from the deepest part of my heart. Now, let's dive back into our journey to high self-esteem.

Your biggest supporter, Daniel Powers

PS - Did you know? When you offer something valuable to someone else, you become more valuable in their eyes. If you think this book can help another person like it helped you, consider sharing it with them.

BUILDING BONDS: THE ESSENCE OF SISTERHOOD

A tapestry, rich and complex, gains its strength not from individual threads but from the myriad ways they intertwine, creating a resilient and beautiful fabric. This analogy mirrors the intricate web of relationships that form the crux of women's support networks, a testament to the power of collective strength and shared experiences. Within this web, the essence of sisterhood shines as a beacon of support, empowerment, and belonging, offering a sanctuary where self-esteem flourishes, nurtured by the bonds of understanding and mutual respect.

THE POWER OF SISTERHOOD: FINDING YOUR TRIBE

Community as a Foundation

At the heart of human connection lies the innate need for belonging, a pillar upon which the edifice of self-esteem rests. For women, the quest for a supportive community—a tribe that resonates with one's values and aspirations—becomes a vital endeavor. This search is not merely about finding a group of like-minded individuals but about discovering a collective where one can truly belong, where the vulnerabilities and strengths of each member are met with empathy and acceptance. Studies, such as those highlighted by the American Psychological Association, affirm the positive correlation between belonging to such communities and enhanced self-esteem, underscoring the foundational role of sisterhood in women's psychological well-being.

Identifying Your Tribe

Finding one's tribe necessitates a journey of self-reflection and exploration, a mindful assessment of one's values, interests, and aspirations. It might begin in the quiet corners of local book clubs, in the lively discussions of community workshops, or amongst the fervent activism of local advocacy groups. The key lies in seeking spaces where one's passions and pursuits align with those of the collective, where the exchange of ideas and support flows freely. A practical approach involves listing personal interests and values, followed by research into local or online groups that cater to these areas. Engaging in these spaces, whether attending meetings or participating in online forums, offers insights into the group dynamics, allowing one to gauge the level of resonance and belonging.

The Benefits of Sisterhood

The unique benefits of female support networks manifest in myriad ways, from the deep sense of understanding from shared experiences to the empowerment that arises from collective achievement. Sisterhood provides a mirror in which we see reflected not only our individual worth but also the collective power of women uplifting women. This network acts as a safety net, a place of refuge during times of turmoil, and a source of celebration during moments of triumph. It fosters an environment where self-esteem is supported and actively cultivated through recognizing and affirming each member's worth and contributions.

Engaging with Your Community

Active engagement in one's community strengthens the bonds of sisterhood, enriching both the individual and the collective. This involvement can take various forms, from participating in community projects and events to supporting fellow members during challenging times. Volunteering for leadership roles or initiating new programs within the group amplifies one's contribution, enhancing the sense of belonging and self-worth. Additionally, creating spaces for open dialogue, where members can share their successes and struggles, fosters a culture of transparency and mutual support. Such engagement bolsters the community and reinforces one's identity within the tribe, solidifying the foundations upon which self-esteem is built.

Visual Element: Sisterhood Circle Guidelines

A detailed infographic titled "Sisterhood Circle Guidelines" offers a visual roadmap for creating and nurturing supportive female networks. Divided into segments such as "Building Trust," "Fostering Open Communication," "Celebrating Diversity," and "Supporting Growth," each section provides actionable steps for cultivating a thriving community. For instance, under "Building Trust," suggestions include regular meet-ups, confidentiality agreements, and empathy exercises to create a safe and supportive environment. This infographic is a practical tool for those seeking to join or create a sisterhood circle, encapsulating the core principles underpinning successful women's networks.

In this exploration of the power of sisterhood, the analogy of the tapestry returns, reminding us that the strength and beauty of our lives are enriched by the threads of connection that bind us. Sisterhood offers a sanctuary where self-esteem is protected and actively nurtured, where the bonds of empathy, understanding, and mutual respect weave a fabric of unparalleled support. Within this fabric, we find our tribe, a community that not only reflects our values and aspirations but also amplifies our strength, resilience, and capacity for joy. The journey to find and engage with one's tribe, while varied and personal, is underscored by the universal truth that in sisterhood, we find not just belonging but a wellspring of empowerment that elevates us all.

MENTORSHIP AND GROWTH: LEARNING FROM OTHERS

In the intricate dance of personal and professional evolution, mentors emerge as pivotal guides, illuminating paths previously shrouded in uncertainty and fostering growth with wisdom gleaned from experience. The mentor-mentee relationship, a dynamic interplay of guidance, support, and shared ambition, is a testament to the transformative power of learning from those who have navigated the waters we currently traverse. This bond, rooted in trust and mutual respect, transcends mere knowledge transfer, embedding itself in the core of our developmental journey, enriching both the giver and the receiver of wisdom.

The Role of Mentors

With their reservoirs of experience, mentors serve not only as navigators but also as mirrors, reflecting our potential often obscured by self-doubt or inexperience. Their insights, born from successes and setbacks, provide a compass by which we can steer our course, avoiding pitfalls while seizing opportunities with a heightened sense of purpose. Beyond the pragmatic wisdom on navigating professional landscapes, mentors imbue us with the confidence to stretch beyond our perceived limitations, fostering a belief in our affirming and transformative capabilities. This formal or informal mentorship becomes a conduit through which ambition is nurtured, resilience is built, and possibilities are expanded, setting the stage for a journey marked by continuous growth and self-discovery.

Finding a Mentor

Like seeking a lighthouse in a vast sea, the quest for a mentor requires clarity of purpose and an openness to exploration. It begins with a deep introspection of one's goals, aspirations, and areas of desired growth, forming a blueprint that guides the search. Casting the net wide, from professional networks to industry forums, one seeks out individuals whose career trajectories resonate with one's aspirations and whose ethos aligns with one's values. Approaching potential mentors demands courage, genuine curiosity, and respect for their journey. A well-crafted outreach, whether through a thoughtful email or a connection at a professional event, should articulate admiration for their accomplishments and a clear vision of what one seeks to learn from the relationship. It's a delicate balance between expressing earnest ambition and recognizing the value of their time and wisdom, an invitation for them to play a pivotal role in one's growth narrative.

Being a Mentee

The art of being a mentee, a role as proactive as it is receptive, hinges on engagement, initiative, and reflection. This role demands more than passive absorption of wisdom; it calls for active participation in the learning process and an eagerness to apply insights and seek feedback with an openness to constructive critique. Setting clear goals for the mentorship, coupled with regular check-ins, ensures the relationship remains aligned with evolving aspirations. Preparing for meetings with specific questions or updates on progress demonstrates respect for the mentor's time and a commitment to maximizing the value of the exchange. Embracing vulnerability and sharing challenges and successes enriches the mentorship with depth, fostering a connection that transcends professional guidance to touch the core of personal growth.

The Reciprocal Nature of Mentorship

At its zenith, mentorship embodies reciprocity, a symbiotic exchange where growth and enrichment flow in both directions. For mentors, engaging with mentees' fresh perspectives and vibrant ambition reinvigorates their passion, offering a reflective space to revisit their journey through the lens of mentorship. This interaction, a melding of experiences and aspirations, often sparks innovation, challenges complacency, and renews a sense of purpose in their professional endeavors. Mentees, in turn, gain not just guidance but also the opportunity to contribute to their mentor's narrative, perhaps by offering insights into emerging trends or new technologies. This reciprocal flow of value underscores the profound impact of mentorship, elevating it from a mere transfer of knowledge to a dynamic relationship that enriches both participants, enhancing self-esteem and expanding the realms of possibility for mentor and mentee alike.

In exploring mentorship and growth, the narrative unfolds as a celebration of shared wisdom, a journey where learning from others transcends knowledge acquisition to become a transformative experience. Through the guidance of mentors, the proactive engagement of mentees, and the reciprocal enrichment of the mentorship bond, individuals navigate the complexities of personal and professional growth with a heightened sense of purpose. This dynamic interplay of guidance, support, and shared ambition fosters individual evolution and strengthens the fabric of communities, creating a legacy of growth and learning that transcends generations.

ONLINE COMMUNITIES: VIRTUAL SUPPORT NETWORKS

The advent and proliferation of digital platforms have necessitated a reevaluation of how connections are formed, nurtured, and sustained. With this modern paradigm, online communities have burgeoned, offering havens where individuals, irrespective of geographical constraints, can unite over shared experiences, interests, and challenges. These virtual congregations have become increasingly indispensable, providing support and connection in a world where physical distances sometimes render traditional support networks less accessible.

The Rise of Online Communities

In the digital age, the creation and expansion of online communities have marked a significant shift in the landscape of social interaction. Platforms ranging from forums and social media groups to specialized apps have facilitated the congregation of individuals around virtually every conceivable interest or concern. This phenomenon is a testament to the internet's capacity to connect people and reflects a deeper, more profound human yearning for connection, understanding, and a sense of belonging. The significance of these virtual spaces lies in their ability to offer solace, advice, and camaraderie, transcending the barriers of physical distance to create a fabric of support as real and tangible as that found in physical communities.

Navigating Virtual Spaces

Finding and integrating oneself into online communities that are positive, supportive, and aligned with one's aspirations requires both discernment and strategy. The initial step involves identifying platforms that resonate with one's interests or needs, a task that benefits from the specificity of goals and the clarity of intent. Upon pinpointing these digital havens, active participation becomes vital. Engaging in meaningful discussions, sharing insights, and offering support to others can elevate one's presence from a mere observer to a valued community member. However, truly benefiting from these spaces lies in the quality of interactions rather than the quantity. Fostering genuine connections, even in the digital realm, necessitates a willingness to be open and respectful, contributing to the community's collective wisdom while gaining insights and support.

Safety and Authenticity Online

While the anonymity of the internet offers a veil behind which individuals can freely express themselves, it also presents challenges to safety and authenticity. Engaging in online communities necessitates a vigilant approach to personal information and a discerning eye toward the authenticity of others. Adopting pseudonyms or avatars can offer a layer of protection, allowing for exploring sensitive topics without exposing oneself to potential risks. Equally, assessing the authenticity and intentions of fellow community members benefits from a cautious approach, especially in spaces where support and vulnerability intersect. Critical evaluation of the advice shared, and the sources behind it ensure that one's foray into virtual support networks remains safe and beneficial. Within this careful balance of openness and caution, authentic connections can flourish, rooted in mutual respect and a shared commitment to creating a safe space for all members.

The Impact of Online Support

The influence of virtual support networks on self-esteem and personal growth is profound and multifaceted. For many, these digital spaces offer the first glimpse into a world where their experiences are validated, their feelings acknowledged, and their challenges met with empathy and understanding. The support garnered in these communities can act as a catalyst for personal development, bolstering self-esteem through recognizing and appreciating one's worth by peers. Moreover, the insights and perspectives gained from these virtual interactions can complement real-life connections, offering new strategies for coping, enhancing resilience, and fostering a more nuanced understanding of one's self and others. Online communities can serve as bridges, connecting individuals to more comprehensive support networks and resources that might otherwise remain beyond reach.

The sphere of online communities emerges not merely as a feature of the digital age but as a cornerstone of modern support systems. These virtual spaces, with their unique ability to unite individuals across divides, promise understanding, growth, and connection. They reaffirm the enduring human capacity to seek out and foster bonds of support, underscoring that, even in an increasingly digitized world, the need for community, empathy, and shared experience remains as vital as ever.

THE ROLE OF FRIENDSHIP IN SELF-ESTEEM BUILDING

In the intricate mosaic of human relationships, friends act as both a mirror and a scaffold, reflecting our intrinsic value while lifting us toward our potential. This dual role underscores friendships' profound impact on our self-image and overall sense of worth. Within these bonds, we find not just reflection but affirmation, a resonant echo of our virtues and strengths that bolsters our self-esteem.

Friends as Mirrors

The reflection friends offer transcends mere mimicry, serving instead as a nuanced portrayal of our essence. In their eyes, we catch glimpses of ourselves stripped of the usual veneer of self-criticism, beholding qualities we might overlook or undervalue. This mirroring, imbued with affection and respect, provides a corrective lens to our self-perception, challenging the distortions wrought by our inner critic. It's in the laughter shared over past follies, the comfort offered in moments of vulnerability, and the unabashed celebration of our triumphs that friends affirm our worth, reinforcing a positive self-image that becomes a bulwark against the erosive forces of doubt and insecurity.

Cultivating Healthy Friendships

The cultivation of healthy friendships, those characterized by mutual respect, understanding, and support, requires intention and discernment. Qualities such as empathy, honesty, and a genuine desire for the other's well-being form the bedrock of these relationships. Like gardeners tending to a cherished plot, we must nurture these bonds with the sustenance of time, the water of shared experiences, and the sunlight of positive interaction. Communication, primarily, serves as a vital nutrient, ensuring misunderstandings are swiftly uprooted, and the soil of companionship remains fertile. In selecting the seeds of new friendships, an awareness of these qualities guides us toward connections that promise reciprocal growth and enrichment.

Navigating Friendships at Different Life Stages

As life's seasons shift, so does the landscape of friendships, evolving to reflect the changing contours of our needs, circumstances, and understandings. Childhood friends, with whom we navigated the initial explorations of identity and belonging, may give way to or be joined by bonds formed in the crucible of adolescence, college, or early adulthood, each stage bringing forth its own challenges and revelations. This evolution, while natural, tests the resilience and adaptability of friendships, demanding flexibility that allows the relationship to blossom in new soil. The transition from one life stage to another often acts as a sieve, distinguishing fleeting connections from those rooted in a more profound synchronicity of spirit. Acknowledging and embracing this dynamic nature of friendships ensures that our support networks remain vibrant and reflect our journey, enhancing self-esteem through each phase of life.

The Importance of Reciprocity

At its core, the vitality of friendship lies in the principle of reciprocity, a balanced exchange where support, understanding, and affection flow freely in both directions. This mutual nourishment, a give-and-take that transcends the transactional, fosters a sense of equity and value within the relationship. Reciprocity ensures that both parties feel seen, heard, and appreciated, their contributions recognized, and their needs met with sensitivity and care. Within this equilibrium, friendships thrive, becoming sources of joy, strength, and affirmation. The act of giving, whether in the form of time, attention, or support, becomes as enriching to the giver as to the receiver, a testament to the synergistic potential of human connection.

In the realm of friendships, we discover a powerful ally in the quest for self-esteem, a dynamic interplay of reflection, affirmation, and mutual growth that fortifies our sense of self. These relationships, nurtured with intention and care, evolve alongside us, mirroring our journey while contributing to the scaffolding upon which we build a resilient and positive self-image. By cultivating healthy, reciprocal friendships, we ensure that our support network remains a wellspring of strength, capable of withstanding the vicissitudes of life while enhancing our capacity for joy and fulfillment.

As we turn our gaze towards the horizon, the lessons gleaned from the bonds of friendship illuminate the path forward, offering strategies and insights that apply not just to personal relationships but to the broader spectrum of human interaction. In understanding the foundational role of friendships in self-esteem building, we are equipped with the tools to navigate the complexities of connection, empathy, and mutual support, principles that underpin the rich tapestry of our social fabric. This understanding, rooted in the value of reciprocity and the transformative power of shared growth, paves the way for a deeper exploration of human dynamics, setting the stage for the continued journey toward self-discovery and collective empowerment.

COMMUNICATION AND CONNECTION: THE PILLARS OF SELF-ESTEEM

In a world where voices clamor for attention, from the cacophony of social media to the whispers of our innermost thoughts, finding and asserting one's true voice emerges as a profound act of self-assurance. In the nuanced dance of expressing our truth, we discover the core of our self-esteem—not in the echoes of what others want to hear, but in the resonance of our authentic selves. This chapter unfolds the tapestry of communication as a foundational element of self-esteem, exploring the intricate patterns formed by honesty, vulnerability, and the courage to confront judgment.

SPEAKING YOUR TRUTH: COMMUNICATION FOR SELF-ESTEEM

Honesty and Authenticity

The cornerstone of meaningful communication lies in the bedrock of honesty and authenticity. Like a tree rooted in fertile soil, our words gain strength from the depth of our sincerity, growing branches that reach out and connect with others in genuine interaction. In personal relationships, honesty cultivates trust, weaving a bond strengthened by the assurance of truth. Authenticity, meanwhile, serves as a mirror reflecting our innermost selves, inviting others to see us as we are, not as facades molded by expectation or desire. This dual commitment to honesty and authenticity fortifies relationships and nurtures self-respect, affirming our value in being truthfully seen and heard.

Finding Your Voice

The journey to finding one's voice often begins in the quiet introspection of our thoughts and feelings, a landscape rich with the nuances of our experiences. To confidently express these thoughts and feelings requires practice, akin to a musician tuning an instrument, finding the right pitch that resonates with clarity and purpose. One practical method involves journaling, a space where thoughts can flow unencumbered by external judgment, allowing for exploring and articulating our inner dialogue. Another avenue is participation in discussion groups or forums, where the exchange of ideas offers a platform to refine and assert our voice in the company of others, fostering a sense of belonging and self-assurance.

The Power of Vulnerability

Often shrouded in fear and misconception, vulnerability is vital to deepening connections, a bridge to understanding and empathy. Brené Brown, a renowned researcher on the subject, describes vulnerability as "the birthplace of love, belonging, joy, courage, empathy, and creativity." In the moments we dare to share our fears, hopes, and dreams, we invite others into our world, creating a space where the shared courage of openness fortifies connections. Embracing vulnerability in communication enhances self-esteem and encourages others to reciprocate, fostering a cycle of mutual trust and understanding.

Overcoming the Fear of Judgment

The specter of judgment often looms large, casting shadows of doubt over our willingness to speak our truth. Overcoming this fear begins with the recognition that the opinions of others, while valuable, do not define our worth. Strategies to navigate this fear include:

- Reframing negative feedback as opportunities for growth.
- Setting boundaries around who's input we value.
- Practicing self-compassion.
- Reminding ourselves of our inherent worth regardless of external validation.

Engaging in public speaking workshops or groups, such as Toastmasters, can also provide a supportive environment to practice and build confidence in expressing oneself, diminishing the power judgment holds over our self-expression.

Visual Element: "The Authentic Communication Wheel"

An infographic titled "The Authentic Communication Wheel" offers readers a visual guide to integrating honesty, authenticity, vulnerability, and confidence into their daily interactions. This wheel is segmented into four quadrants, each representing a key aspect of authentic communication, with actionable steps and reflective questions designed to encourage self-exploration and practice. For instance, in the vulnerability quadrant, prompts might include "Share something you're passionate about with someone new," encouraging steps toward openness. This visual tool serves as both a reminder and a roadmap for readers seeking to enrich their communication practices and, by extension, their self-esteem.

Navigating the labyrinth of communication, from unveiling our truths to embracing vulnerability, is an act of self-discovery and assertion that lies at the heart of self-esteem. Through the spoken word, we affirm our presence, our worth, and our connection to the world around us. As we venture forth, let us carry the lessons of honesty, authenticity, and the courage to face judgment, fashioning our path with the clarity of our voices and the strength of our convictions.

LISTENING WITH EMPATHY: BUILDING DEEPER CONNECTIONS

Empathy and active listening intertwine to create a resilient and revealing fabric in the tapestry of human connection. Truly listening, of immersing oneself in another's narrative without the intrusion of one's own judgments or experiences, stands as a profound testament to the human capacity for understanding and compassion. This depth of connection, fostered through the principles of active listening, transforms conversations into bridges, spanning the chasms that often separate us from one another.

The Art of Active Listening

Active listening transcends the passive reception of words, evolving into an engaged and conscious effort to understand the essence of what is being communicated. This form of listening involves a multifaceted engagement: it is the nod of acknowledgment, the mirror of the speaker's emotions reflected in the listener's eyes, and the silence that offers space for unspoken words. Within this practice, the listener becomes an alchemist, transforming the raw material of spoken words into a shared understanding, a mutual respect that validates the speaker's experiences and feelings.

The principles guiding active listening anchor themselves in the presence, an unwavering focus that silences the internal cacophony to attend to the nuances of the speaker's message. Questions, when they arise, serve not to steer the conversation but to delve deeper into the speaker's perspective, illuminating insights that might otherwise remain obscured. Paraphrasing becomes a tool, not of repetition, but of interpretation, a reflection that assures the speaker of their words' impact and comprehension.

Empathy vs. Sympathy

Navigating the subtle yet significant distinction between empathy and sympathy unveils the layers of complexity in human connection. Sympathy, often characterized by a well-intentioned acknowledgment of another's distress, maintains a certain distance, an observer's perspective that offers solace without immersion into the emotional landscape of the other. Empathy, on the other hand, entails a leap into the realm of shared feeling, a willingness to inhabit the emotional world of the speaker, seeing through their eyes and feeling with their heart. This leap does not dilute one's individuality but expands it, embracing the vulnerability that comes with true understanding.

Practicing Empathetic Listening

Cultivating empathetic listening skills demands intentionality, a conscious effort to refine the capacity for deep, empathetic engagement. One practical exercise involves the silent repetition of the speaker's words in the listener's mind, a technique that fosters concentration and discourages premature formulation of responses. Another method, reflective listening, encourages listeners to articulate their understanding of the speaker's message, offering a summary that captures what has been communicated. This practice not only validates the speaker's experience but also encourages a dialogue that is rooted in mutual comprehension and respect.

Role-playing exercises enhance empathetic listening by simulating scenarios requiring participants to alternate between speaking and listening roles. These simulations, set within a framework that encourages feedback and reflection, illuminate the challenges and triumphs of striving for empathy in communication. Such exercises sharpen listening skills and foster an environment where empathy is practiced and celebrated.

The Benefits of Being Heard

At the core of the human experience lies a fundamental desire to be understood and acknowledged. Feeling heard has manifold psychological benefits, impacting both the speaker and the listener in profound ways. For the speaker, sharing one's thoughts and emotions in a space where they are not only heard but understood fosters a sense of validation and self-worth. This validation, when received from a place of empathy and nonjudgment, can catalyze healing, encourage self-exploration, and strengthen the bonds of connection.

Empathetic listening opens doors to previously unseen worlds for the listener, offering insights into the lives and experiences of others that enrich one's understanding of the human condition. This expansion of perspective enhances one's capacity for compassion and nurtures a sense of interconnectedness, a recognition of the shared vulnerabilities and triumphs that define us. The reciprocity inherent in this exchange, where understanding is both given and received, creates a foundation for lasting, meaningful relationships.

In communication, active listening and empathy are not mere techniques but expressions of a deeper commitment to understanding and connection. They are the threads that weave the fabric of human relationships, binding us in a shared narrative of compassion and mutual respect. Through the diligent application of these principles, we not only bridge the gaps that divide us but also discover the profound joy and fulfillment that comes from truly connecting with one another.

ASSERTIVENESS TRAINING: EXPRESSING YOURSELF WITH CONFIDENCE

In the intricate dance of interpersonal relations, assertiveness emerges as a pivotal skill, a golden mean between the extremes of aggression and passivity. It is the voice of self-assuredness that allows one to stake a claim in the world and affirm one's needs, opinions, and boundaries without infringing on the rights of others. This delicate yet powerful equilibrium offers the key to unlocking relationships that thrive on mutual respect and understanding, fostering an environment where self-esteem can flourish unabated.

Understanding Assertiveness

Assertiveness is often misconceived, tangled in the web of misconceptions that equate it with aggressiveness. Yet, at its core, assertiveness is the embodiment of balance. It is the ability to communicate one's thoughts, feelings, and needs directly and appropriately, standing firm in one's convictions while remaining empathetic to the perspectives of others. Unlike aggression, which seeks to dominate and win at the expense of another, assertiveness operates from a platform of equality. It acknowledges the validity of differing viewpoints without surrendering one's own. Similarly, it distances itself from passivity, which, in its avoidance of conflict, often suppresses one's voice and needs. By navigating these waters with precision and care, assertiveness fosters a climate where dialogue flourishes and relationships deepen, anchored in the authenticity of shared truths.

The Importance of Assertive Communication

The significance of assertive communication in the tapestry of human connections cannot be overstated. It acts as a linchpin, securing the foundations of honest and satisfying interactions. In personal relationships, assertiveness paves the way for open and transparent exchanges, where expectations are voiced and misunderstandings are swiftly addressed. This transparency mitigates the potential for conflict and reinforces the bonds of trust and intimacy. Within professional settings, assertiveness is a testament to one's integrity and competence, fostering respect and collaboration. The ripple effects of assertive communication extend into self-esteem, as each act of assertiveness reaffirms one's worth and right to be heard, gradually weaving a more substantial, more resilient fabric of self-assurance.

Techniques for Assertive Communication

The cultivation of assertiveness is akin to mastering an art, requiring both practice and finesse. Techniques for assertive communication are diverse, each tailored to empower individuals to express themselves with clarity and confidence. For instance, using "I" statements allows for expressing thoughts and feelings without attributing blame, reducing the likelihood of defensive reactions. Phrases like "I feel" or "I need" are gateways to open, heartfelt discussions. The technique of fogging, wherein one agrees with any truth in criticism without becoming defensive, acts as a deflector, maintaining one's composure and steering conversations away from potential conflict. Similarly, the broken record technique involves calmly and persistently repeating one's message without escalation, ensuring one's point is acknowledged without resorting to aggression. These tools, among others, equip individuals with the means to navigate a myriad of situations with assurance and poise, asserting their needs while fostering an environment of mutual respect.

Setting Boundaries Through Assertiveness

At the intersection of assertiveness and self-care lies the critical practice of setting boundaries, a manifestation of self-respect, and a declaration of self-worth. Boundaries act as safeguards, demarcating the limits of what is acceptable and tolerable within interpersonal dynamics. Through assertiveness, these boundaries are communicated clearly and respectfully, signaling to others the parameters of engagement. This practice, far from being a barrier to connection, is a cornerstone for healthy, fulfilling relationships. It delineates a space where individuals can interact with freedom and authenticity, secure in knowing their limits are recognized and respected. In articulating these boundaries, whether they pertain to time, emotional capacity, or personal values, assertiveness ensures that they are established and maintained, providing a framework within which relationships can thrive and self-esteem can ascend to new heights.

In the realm of assertiveness, where communication and self-expression converge, lies the potential for transformation. Here, individuals discover the strength to voice their truth, claim their space in the tapestry of human connections, and do so with a confidence that is both empowering and liberating. Through the meticulous application of assertive techniques and the conscious setting of boundaries, the landscape of interpersonal relations is redefined, marked by a depth of understanding, respect, and mutual growth. As we navigate this terrain, armed with the tools of assertiveness, we unlock the doors to more honest, satisfying relationships that are instrumental in the flowering of our self-esteem.

CONFLICT RESOLUTION: NAVIGATING DISAGREEMENTS WITH GRACE

Within the intricate web of human connections, conflict emerges not as an anomaly but as an inherent element woven into the very fabric of our interactions. Acknowledging this reality paves the way for a perspective shift, where conflict is perceived not as a disruptor to be avoided but as an opportunity for growth, deepened understanding, and the fortification of bonds. Within this context, we explore the terrain of conflict resolution, a landscape marked by the delicate balance between self-expression and empathetic engagement, aiming to navigate disagreements with a dignity that honors all involved.

The inevitability of conflict in relationships stems from human experience and perspective diversity. Each individual brings a unique constellation of beliefs, desires, and boundaries to the table, creating a rich tapestry of interaction that, while primarily harmonious, is occasionally prone to friction. Recognizing conflict as a natural occurrence demystifies its presence, allowing us to approach disagreements with a mindset geared toward resolution rather than avoidance or conquest. This normalization encourages a proactive stance, where conflicts are addressed to find mutual ground, thus preserving the integrity and vitality of the relationship.

Strategies for healthy conflict resolution are as varied as the conflicts themselves, yet they share a common foundation in respect, communication, and a genuine desire for harmony. One practical approach involves the practice of reflective listening, where each party takes turns expressing their viewpoint while the other actively listens, refraining from interruption or defense. This technique fosters an environment of mutual respect, where understanding precedes the search for solutions. Another strategy centers on expressing needs and feelings using "I" statements. This method personalizes the impact of the conflict without assigning blame, reducing defensiveness and paving the way for empathetic dialogue.

Compromise stands as a pillar in the architecture of conflict resolution, embodying the principle of give-and-take essential to maintaining healthy relationships. True compromise involves an equitable exchange where the needs and desires of all parties are considered and honored to the greatest extent possible. This process requires flexibility, creativity, and an overarching commitment to the relationship's well-being, qualities that ensure the solutions reached are not only fair but also sustainable. Compromise, in its essence, is a testament to the value placed on the relationship, a willing adjustment of individual positions for collective harmony.

The journey through conflict, guided by understanding, communication, and compromise strategies, invariably leads to a deepening of connections and personal growth. Navigating disagreements with grace transforms potential rifts into opportunities for insight, empathy, and the strengthening of bonds. Through this process, individuals learn not only about the perspectives and needs of others but also about their capacities for patience, forgiveness, and adaptation. When resolved with intention and care, conflicts become milestones in the evolution of relationships and the individuals within them, markers of resilience and mutual respect.

As we conclude this exploration of conflict resolution, it becomes evident that the essence of navigating disagreements lies not in avoiding conflict but in the manner of its engagement. The strategies and perspectives shared herein offer a blueprint for transforming potential discord into opportunities for growth, understanding, and deepening bonds. It is through the graceful handling of disagreements that relationships are preserved and enriched, emerging from the crucible of conflict stronger and more resilient.

In moving forward, let us carry the lessons gleaned from the delicate dance of conflict resolution, embracing the complexities of human interaction with a heart geared toward harmony and growth. As we transition into the subsequent facets of our journey, these insights into resolving conflict serve as a foundation upon which to build connections that are enduring and nurturing, marked by the depth of understanding and mutual respect that characterizes truly meaningful relationships.

DAILY PRACTICES FOR HIGH
SELF-ESTEEM

A canvas blank and unmarred by brushstrokes awakens with the first light of dawn, holding within its fibers the potential for masterpieces or missteps. So, too, does each day offer a fresh tableau to inscribe our intentions, actions, and reflections, a daily resurgence of opportunities to mold our self-esteem with deliberate care. The rituals we engage in from the moment our consciousness stirs from slumber to the last flicker of thought before sleep are the pigments with which we color this canvas, each hue a testament to our commitment to nurturing self-worth and confidence.

MORNING RITUALS FOR A CONFIDENT DAY

Starting with Positivity

The first whispers of dawn, with its gentle light easing the dark's departure, mirror the awakening of our minds, a transition from the vulnerable honesty of dreams to the structured reality of waking life. In these initial moments, the mind, malleable and receptive, presents an optimal ground for planting seeds of positivity. Positive affirmations, simple yet potent declarations of our worth, capabilities, and aspirations, serve as this nourishment. Whispered to a reflection in the mirror or penned in a bedside journal, phrases like "I am capable," "Today, I choose joy," or "I embrace my strength" become mantras that set the tone for self-support and optimism. This practice, rooted in the psychological principle of self-suggestion, leverages the brain's tendency towards confirmation bias, steering our focus towards the constructive and uplifting.

Visualization Techniques

Imagine standing at the threshold of your day, the hours stretched out before you like roads diverging in a wood, each path pregnant with possibilities. Visualization, a technique championed for its efficacy by athletes and performers alike, invites you to traverse these paths in the mind's eye, not as a passive observer but as an active participant in crafting the day's narrative. By vividly picturing the day unfolding with success and confidence, from the triumphant completion of tasks to the serene moments of connection with others, we encode these outcomes into our psyche. This mental rehearsal reinforces our self-esteem and primes us for actualizing these envisioned successes, a preparatory ritual that arms us with purpose and poise.

Mindful Movement

In the symphony of morning rituals, the body, too, demands its crescendo, a physical awakening to match the mind's ascent. Gentle exercise or yoga, practiced with mindfulness, becomes a dialogue between body and soul, each movement a wordless affirmation of our vitality and strength. As the body stretches and strengthens, so does our sense of achievement, grounding us in the present and reminding us of our agency over our well-being. This practice, performed as the world still hums with quiet, not only catalyzes our physical energy but also harmonizes our inner realms, fostering a sense of accomplishment that buoys our self-esteem throughout the day.

Intention Setting

With the foundation of positivity laid, the day calls for direction, a compass to navigate the hours. Setting clear, achievable goals for the day crystallizes our intentions, transforming the nebulous into the tangible. Whether articulated in the quiet reflection of morning's first light or scribbled in a planner, this act delineates our priorities and commitments, offering a focus for directed, self-esteem-boosting activities. Intentions range from the professional, such as completing a project phase, to the personal, like dedicating time to a cherished hobby. By marking these intentions, we assert control over our day, a declaration of our capacity to shape our lives in alignment with our values and aspirations.

Interactive Element: Morning Rituals Checklist

A checklist is provided to aid in crafting a morning ritual that resonates with your unique path to high self-esteem. This interactive tool invites personalization, allowing you to select and sequence activities that align with your goals and preferences. Categories such as Positive Affirmations, Visualization, Mindful Movement, and Intention Setting offer a variety of suggested actions, from writing affirmations to planning a ten-minute yoga flow. This checklist, adaptable and evolving, serves as a guide and a reflection of your commitment to fostering confidence and self-worth from the day's start.

In the delicate art of daily living, our morning rituals emerge as the strokes that begin the narrative of our day, which we have the power to author with intention, courage, and grace. These practices, imbued with the capacity to transform our self-perception and elevate our self-esteem, remind us of the beauty and strength that reside within, awaiting our acknowledgment and nurture. As the day unfolds, let these rituals be the foundation upon which we build a day of purpose, connection, and self-respect, painting our canvas with vibrant hues of confidence and self-assuredness.

JOURNALING FOR SELF-DISCOVERY AND EMPOWERMENT

In the quiet corners of our lives, where the hum of the day's demands fades into a whisper, the act of journaling emerges as a sanctuary. Within the bound pages lies a space for introspection and revelation, a canvas upon which the narrative of self can be both discovered and redefined. This practice, ancient yet ever-pertinent, serves not merely as a repository for thoughts but as a crucible for transformation, where the alchemy of words transmutes the leaden weight of doubts into the gold of understanding and self-assurance.

Exploring Personal Narratives

Within our psyche lie narratives as old as time, tales we have inherited or spun for ourselves, shaping our perception of who we are and what we can become. Some of these stories, wrought from the threads of past experiences and societal messages, bind us in a cocoon of limiting beliefs, hindering our flight into the realms of possibility. Journaling offers a means to unravel these narratives, to hold them up to the light, and to discern truth from fiction. By writing our stories, we become both author and audience, gaining the perspective needed to edit and rewrite the scripts that confine us. This process, iterative and reflective, empowers us to author a narrative of our self that resonates with our deepest truths, fostering a foundation of self-esteem built not on the sands of external validation but on the bedrock of authentic self-recognition.

Gratitude Entries

Amidst the tumult of daily existence, the moments of beauty and joy, though plentiful, often slip through our fingers like grains of sand, unnoticed and unacknowledged. To document gratitude is to weave a net fine enough to catch these moments, to collect them in the reservoir of our consciousness where they can nourish and sustain us. The act of noting down the facets of our lives for which we are thankful, from the monumental to the mundane, shifts our gaze from what is lacking to what is abundant. This shift, subtle yet profound, alters the landscape of our minds, cultivating a terrain rich with positivity and resilience. Gratitude, chronicled with intention and regularity, becomes a beacon that guides us back to our core of strength and worth, illuminating the path to self-esteem with the light of appreciation and contentment.

Achievement Tracking

In the rush of relentless forward motion, our achievements, those milestones of effort and success, often blur into the background, their significance dimmed by the next looming goal. To keep a log of accomplishments, both daily victories and long-term triumphs, is to create a map of our journey, a visual testament to our progress and resilience. This record, diligently maintained, serves as a mirror reflecting our capabilities and strengths, a counter-narrative to the voice of self-doubt that whispers of inadequacy. Recording these small and significant successes reinforces our belief in our potential and fortitude, bolstering our self-esteem with concrete evidence of our capacity to overcome challenges and realize our aspirations.

Emotional Processing

The landscape of our emotional lives, vast and varied, holds within its bounds peaks of joy and valleys of sorrow, territories as yet uncharted and realms long familiar. Journaling provides a compass for this exploration, a means to navigate the complexities of our feelings with curiosity and compassion. By articulating our emotions on paper, we externalize them, creating a space where they can be observed, understood, and processed. This externalization allows us to engage with our emotions without being overwhelmed, recognize their transience, and glean the insights they offer. Through journaling, we cultivate a dialogue with ourselves that is both nurturing and healing, a conversation that fosters self-understanding and compassion. This deepened relationship with our emotional selves lays the groundwork for resilient self-esteem rooted in a profound acceptance and appreciation of our full, multifaceted humanity.

Journaling is a testament to the power of words to heal, reveal, and empower in the stillness of reflection. This simple yet profound act becomes a cornerstone of self-discovery and empowerment through the exploration of personal narratives, the practice of gratitude, the tracking of achievements, and the processing of emotions. Each entry, a step toward understanding and acceptance, weaves a narrative of our self, grounded in reality and aspirational in its reach, where self-esteem blossoms in the fertile soil of introspection and authenticity.

THE POWER OF GRATITUDE IN CULTIVATING SELF-WORTH

In the garden of the self, where seeds of potential and growth intertwine with weeds of doubt and despair, gratitude stands as both sunlight and rain, essential elements nurturing the delicate blooms of self-worth. This ritual, far from a mere recitation of thanks, is an active cultivation of awareness, an attuning of the mind to the abundance that permeates even the most mundane aspects of existence. Through this lens, the world transforms, and with it, our place within it, as we recognize our value and contributions not as incidental, but integral to the tapestry of life.

Weaving gratitude into the fabric of our daily lives begins with intention, a conscious decision to seek out and acknowledge each moment's myriad gifts. This might manifest as a quiet reflection over morning coffee, savoring the warmth and richness of the brew, or a silent acknowledgment of the comfort and security provided by our homes at day's end. Each acknowledgment and moment of thanks act as a counterweight to tendencies toward negativity and lack, shifting the balance towards a perception of life as rich and replete with gifts. This shift is not illusory but rooted in gratitude's profound psychological impact on our perception of the world and ourselves within it. Studies, such as those emerging from positive psychology, underscore this transformation, illustrating how gratitude enhances mood, fosters resilience, and, most crucially, bolsters self-esteem by reinforcing a sense of worthiness and belonging.

The sharing of gratitude amplifies its effects, creating ripples that extend beyond the self to touch the lives of others. In expressing appreciation for the large and small acts that enrich our days, we not only affirm the value of these contributions but also reinforce our connections with those around us. This might unfold in a heartfelt note to a colleague, acknowledging their support in a challenging project, or a spontaneous compliment to a stranger, recognizing their kindness. These exchanges, marked by sincerity and openness, not only uplift the recipients but also reinforce our self-esteem as we identify ourselves as agents of positivity and connection. Giving thanks becomes a bridge, fostering relationships built on mutual appreciation and respect, where self-worth is continuously affirmed through positive interactions.

Yet, gratitude reveals its true power in moments of joy and abundance and, perhaps most importantly, in the crucible of challenge. In the shadow of adversity, gratitude acts as a beacon, guiding us toward slivers of light amidst the darkness. Finding things to be grateful for in difficult times requires resilience, a deep-rooted belief in the presence of good even when it seems obscured. This might manifest in the appreciation of a friend's unwavering presence during periods of loss, the recognition of our own strength in navigating hardships, or the simple acknowledgment of a meal shared in solace. These moments of gratitude, hard-won and deeply felt, do more than buoy our spirits; they fortify our self-esteem, reminding us of our resilience, our capacity for connection, and our inherent value, even, and especially, when circumstances test our resolve.

Gratitude emerges not as a passive state but as a dynamic practice, a choice to focus on abundance over lack, connection over isolation, and growth over stagnation. It is a practice that demands mindfulness, the willingness to see beyond immediate circumstances, and the wealth of positivity that life offers. In this choice lies liberation, the freedom to define our worth not by our possessions or achievements but by the depth of our appreciation for the myriad gifts that life bestows, from the exquisite to the seemingly insignificant. Through gratitude, we anchor our self-esteem in the fertile ground of abundance, cultivating a sense of expansive and deeply rooted worth, resistant to the erosive forces of negativity and doubt.

Cultivating gratitude develops us, nurturing a self-worth that thrives on recognition of the good within and around us. This practice, a weaving of thanks into the fabric of our being, transforms our perspective, relationships, and self-perception, revealing that our worth is inherent, immutable, and infinitely worthy of celebration.

EVENING REFLECTIONS: ENDING THE DAY ON A POSITIVE NOTE

In the gentle embrace of twilight, when the day's hustle dissolves into the calm of impending night, our minds, too, segue from the cacophony of tasks and interactions into a reflective repose. This period, nestled between the day's end and night's deep solace, presents a pristine opportunity for introspection—a time to sift through the hours past, distilling wisdom and solace from the day's experiences. The ritual of nightly reflection becomes not just an act of recollection but a deliberate cultivation of self-awareness and esteem, a moment to acknowledge our journey through the day with grace and gratitude.

Reflective Practice

Nightly reflection, as a practice, invites us to hold a mirror to our day, examining its contours with an eye both critical and kind. This process, while reflective, need not dwell solely on introspection's sake but aims to recognize our daily achievements and learnings. By setting aside time each evening to ponder the day's events, decisions, and interactions, we dialogue with our inner selves, unearthing insights that might otherwise fade with the day's close. This act, performed in the hush of evening, becomes a bridge connecting our experiences to our growth, a quiet but potent acknowledgment of our journey's significance.

Celebrating Small Wins

Amid this evening ritual lies the crucial practice of celebrating small victories. Each day, regardless of its grandeur or mundanity, is sprinkled with moments of triumph—tasks completed, kindnesses extended, challenges surmounted. Acknowledging these wins, however minor they seem, reinforces our sense of accomplishment and worth. It's a reaffirmation of our efficacy and resilience, a nod to the incremental but inexorable progress we make each day. This celebration, infused with gratitude for our efforts and achievements, nourishes our self-esteem, reminding us of our capability and strength even in the face of adversity.

Preparing for Rest

As the reflections of the day give way to the anticipation of night's rest, our thoughts, too, must transition. Cultivating positive, self-affirming thoughts as we prepare for sleep is pivotal in setting the tone for restful slumber and a hopeful morrow. By consciously directing our focus towards thoughts that uplift and reassure us, we weave a tapestry of serenity that envelops our minds, easing the transition into sleep. This practice, akin to a lullaby for the soul, prepares us not just for a night of physical rest but for the rejuvenation of our self-esteem, ensuring that we greet the new day not just with rested bodies but with spirits buoyed by a sense of self-worth and optimism.

Letting Go of Negativity

The final thread in the tapestry of our evening ritual involves the release of negativity—those thoughts, worries, and regrets that cling to our consciousness, shadowing our sense of self. Techniques for this release vary, from the written expulsion of concerns onto paper, a symbolic unburdening that frees the mind, to guided meditation, where each breath becomes a vehicle for release. The essence of this practice lies in its intentionality, the conscious choice not to carry the weight of the day's negativity into the sanctity of our rest. By shedding these burdens, we protect and nurture our self-esteem, allowing our evening ritual's positive reflections and affirmations to take root in fertile ground.

In weaving these practices into the fabric of our evenings, we do more than mark the day's close; we honor our journey through it. Reflective practice, celebration of small wins, preparation for rest, and release of negativity become rituals and acts of self-care that affirm our worth and foster our growth. In the quiet of the night, they remind us of our resilience, achievements, and capacity for positivity, laying the foundation for a robust and reflective self-esteem.

As we turn the page on the day, these evening reflections serve as a gentle but powerful reminder of the beauty inherent in our daily journey. They anchor us in the present, even as they prepare us for the morrow, ensuring that each day is lived and cherished, its lessons learned, and its joys acknowledged. This practice, simple in its execution but profound in its impact, reinforces the pillars of self-esteem upon which our sense of self rests, leading us into the night with hearts light and spirits serene, ready to embrace the endless possibilities that each new dawn brings.

LIVING AUTHENTICALLY

In the mosaic of life, each piece, colored by our choices, beliefs, and interactions, contributes to the overarching picture of our existence. Amidst this complex interplay, discovering and adhering to our true self emerges as a silent rebellion against the cacophony of societal expectations and norms. While often challenging, this fidelity to authenticity paves the way for a richness of life marked not by conformity but by the vivid hues of individuality and self-satisfaction.

DISCOVERING YOUR TRUE SELF: BEYOND SOCIAL EXPECTATIONS

Self-Exploration

The road to discovering one's true self meanders through the landscapes of our past experiences, present engagements, and future aspirations. It beckons for a pause, a moment of introspection amidst the relentless forward motion of daily life. Consider the journaling activity not as a mere diary of events but as a reflective practice where questions like "When do I feel most alive?" or "What values resonate deeply with me?" act as lanterns illuminating the path to self-understanding. This process, akin to an archaeologist meticulously uncovering relics of the past, enables us to sift through the sediment of external influences and unearth the bedrock of our authentic selves.

Identifying Core Values

Core values, the compass by which we navigate the seas of life, offer clarity and direction amidst the fog of societal pressures. Identifying these values requires more than a superficial acknowledgment; it demands a deep dive into the waters of self-reflection. A practical approach involves listing activities, people, and experiences that bring joy and fulfillment, then distilling from these the underlying values they represent. When done with honesty and openness, this exercise reveals the constellation of principles that guide our decisions and actions, providing a blueprint for a life of integrity and authenticity.

Challenging Social Norms

The act of challenging social norms, though daunting, is a testament to the strength of one's conviction in the pursuit of authenticity. It involves questioning the status quo, not with the aim of defiance for defiance's sake, but as a means of aligning one's life with one's true self. A real-life application could be the decision to pursue a career path fueled by passion rather than prestige, a choice that, while potentially met with skepticism, aligns with one's value of fulfillment over financial gain. While possibly solitary at its inception, this stance often serves as a beacon for others, inspiring them to also seek alignment between their lives and values.

Authenticity as Freedom

Living authentically, in its essence, is an act of liberation. It frees one from the confines of societal expectations, allowing for a life rich with personal satisfaction and self-esteem. This liberation does not imply a journey devoid of challenges, but rather, it promises a journey true to one's essence, marked by growth, fulfillment, and the profound peace of self-alignment. The feeling of freedom that accompanies authenticity is akin to the sensation of breathing deeply after a prolonged period of constriction, a profound expansion of the self that touches every aspect of life.

Visual Element: The Authenticity Map

A detailed infographic titled "The Authenticity Map" provides a visual guide to navigating the journey towards living authentically. This map charts the terrain from self-exploration to the challenging of social norms, with signposts marking the milestones of identifying core values and embracing authenticity. Each section of the map includes practical steps, reflective questions, and quotes from individuals who have embraced their true selves, serving as both inspiration and guidance. This visual tool, designed to be both practical and inspirational, acts as a companion on the path to authenticity, offering direction and support as one navigates the complexities of aligning life with one's true essence.

In the pursuit of authenticity, we embark on a path less trodden, marked by the courage to confront and transcend societal expectations in favor of a life that resonates deeply with our true selves. Though fraught with challenges, this journey offers unparalleled rewards:

- The freedom to express our individuality.
- The peace that comes from living in alignment with our core values.
- The profound satisfaction of building a life that reflects our most authentic selves.

Through self-exploration, identification of core values, questioning of social norms, and embracing authenticity, we forge a path toward personal fulfillment and self-esteem grounded in the unshakeable foundation of knowing and being true to ourselves.

ALIGNING ACTIONS WITH VALUES: THE INTEGRITY OF SELF-ESTEEM

Value-Based Decision Making

In the labyrinth of life's decisions, where paths fork and twist under the shadow of uncertainty, anchoring oneself to the bedrock of personal core values offers direction and clarity. Making choices that resonate with these deeply held beliefs acts as a beacon, guiding through the fog of societal pressures and fleeting desires. This alignment, however, demands more than mere recognition of one's values; it calls for an integration into the very fabric of daily decision-making. Envision sitting at the crossroads of a significant life choice, the weight of potential outcomes resting heavily on your shoulders. In this moment, drawing upon your values as a compass involves:

- Pausing
- Reflecting on the essence of these guiding principles
- Projecting the potential decisions through the lens of these values

Will this choice amplify my commitment to kindness, to growth, to authenticity? Consulting one's values in such moments transforms decision-making from a task of pros and cons to an act of self-honoring, reinforcing self-esteem with each step taken in alignment with one's true self.

Consistency Between Words and Actions

The tapestry of self-esteem is delicately woven with threads of consistency, where the alignment between proclaimed values and enacted behaviors forms the pattern of integrity. This unity, easy to extol yet challenging to embody, demands vigilance and commitment. It involves a continuous self-audit, a conscious monitoring of the alignment between what we profess and how we act. Imagine the dissonance experienced when actions betray words, the inner turmoil stirred when deeds do not mirror beliefs. This discord not only erodes trust in oneself but also diminishes one's esteem in the eyes of others. Cultivating consistency is not merely an exercise in reliability but a foundational practice in building and maintaining self-esteem. It requires an honest assessment of actions and motivations, ensuring they are not disparate melodies but harmonious chords in the symphony of self.

Handling Discrepancies

Amidst the pursuit of alignment, discrepancies between values and actions inevitably surface, like cracks in a well-crafted vase, marring the integrity of self-esteem. These moments, fraught with self-doubt and guilt, offer fertile ground not for self-flagellation but for growth. Addressing these gaps starts with acknowledgment and a willingness to face the discomfort of misalignment without the shield of denial. From this place of honesty, the path to realignment unfolds through reflection, understanding the roots of the discrepancy, and crafting a plan for reconciliation. Suppose a value of compassion sits at odds with an action driven by anger or impatience. The process of realignment might involve:

- Exploring the triggers of such behavior.
- Seeking forgiveness from oneself and those affected.
- Implementing strategies to respond more congruently in the future.

This approach, centered on accountability and learning, transforms potential pitfalls into stepping stones, reinforcing self-esteem through resilience and a commitment to personal growth.

Living with Integrity

The essence of living with integrity is the embodiment of one's values, not as abstract concepts but as living, breathing aspects of daily existence. This congruence between beliefs and behavior is the heartbeat of self-esteem, a rhythm that pulses with the authenticity of actions taken in harmony with one's true self. Integrity infuses each decision with purpose and each action with meaning, elevating the mundane into expressions of personal truth. It is found in the small acts of kindness that echo a value of compassion, in the steadfast pursuit of truth that reflects a commitment to honesty, and in the boundaries maintained with a gentle firmness that honors respect for oneself and others. This way of living, marked by a steadfast adherence to one's values, nurtures a robust self-esteem fortified against the vicissitudes of life's challenges. It fosters a deep-seated respect for oneself, mirrored in the respect accorded by others, and cultivates a life of satisfaction and fulfillment, rooted in the knowledge that one's existence is an authentic expression of one's deepest truths. In this alignment lies not just the integrity of self-esteem but the very essence of a life lived fully and truly.

THE JOY OF BEING YOU: CELEBRATING YOUR UNIQUE SELF

In the vast expanse of human existence, where each soul meanders through the tapestry of life, marked by distinctive patterns of thought, emotion, and action, the act of embracing one's uniqueness emerges not merely as an act of self-acceptance but as a profound celebration of individuality. This embrace, far from a passive acknowledgment, is an active affirmation of the singular qualities that distinguish one being from another, a recognition that these differences are not flaws but strengths. These intricate threads contribute to the richness of the human mosaic.

Encouraging readers to embrace and celebrate their unique traits necessitates dismantling the pervasive myths that equate uniformity with desirability, a challenging yet vital endeavor. This process begins with a recalibration of perspective, a shift from viewing uniqueness as a divergence to seeing it as a beacon of individuality. Consider the myriad ways in which nature demonstrates diversity: the singular beauty of a snowflake, the distinct melody of a bird's song. These natural phenomena do not seek conformity; instead, they exist in a state of splendid uniqueness. Similarly, recognizing the inherent value in our quirks, from the timbre of our laughter to the eccentricities of our passions, transforms our understanding of self-worth, anchoring it in the authenticity of our being.

The trap of comparison, a labyrinthine pitfall that ensnares many, thrives on the distortion of perspective, magnifying others' highlights while minimizing our own. Overcoming this trap requires a conscious redirection of focus, a pivot from external validation to internal affirmation. Strategies to facilitate this shift include cultivating mindfulness. This awareness anchors us in the reality of our journey, appreciating it for its intrinsic worth rather than measuring it against another's. Additionally, setting personal benchmarks for success and goals that resonate with our values and aspirations liberates us from the comparison cycle, allowing our achievements to stand as testaments to our progress rather than as subjects for comparison.

Introducing practices for regularly celebrating oneself serves as a counterbalance to the often critical internal dialogue that shadows our days. This celebration, manifesting in rituals that honor our growth, achievements, and uniqueness, acts as a salve to the wounds of self-doubt. Simple yet impactful actions, such as a weekly reflection dedicated to acknowledging personal victories or creating a 'brag book, a collection of accolades, positive feedback, and moments of pride, serve as tangible reminders of our worth. These practices, far from selfish, are vital exercises in self-appreciation, reinforcing the belief in our capabilities and worth.

The power of self-love, the keystone in the arch of self-esteem, underpins the joy of being oneself. This form of love, transcending mere acceptance, is an active embrace of all facets of our being, from the light of our strengths to the shadow of our flaws. In this embrace, true freedom lies in the liberty to exist unapologetically as ourselves, unfettered by the chains of pretense or the weight of expectation. Self-love fosters a sanctuary within, a space of unconditional acceptance where the seeds of self-esteem take root and flourish. It nurtures a resilience that buffers against the vicissitudes of external opinion, fortifying our sense of self against the erosive forces of criticism and rejection.

This cultivation of self-love and acceptance is not an endeavor embarked upon in isolation but a process enriched by the waters of community and connection. Surrounding oneself with individuals who recognize and celebrate our uniqueness creates an environment where self-love thrives. These connections, reflecting the beauty of our individuality, reinforce the joy of being oneself, amplifying the resonance of our unique melody in the symphony of human existence.

In navigating the currents of life, where conformity beckons with the allure of acceptance and the fear of divergence looms large, the choice to stand firm in the truth of our uniqueness is both an act of courage and a declaration of self-worth. It is a testament to the belief that the facets of our being, each marked by distinct patterns of thought, emotion, and action, are not mere deviations from the norm but expressions of our individuality, deserving of celebration. This celebration, rooted in embracing uniqueness, overcoming comparison, self-celebration, and cultivating self-love, transforms our journey into a vibrant tapestry of self-acceptance and joy. In this tapestry, the singular beauty of being oneself is acknowledged and revered.

LEAVING A LEGACY: THE IMPACT OF HIGH SELF-ESTEEM ON THE WORLD

High self-esteem is not a lantern held aloft merely to illuminate the individual path but rather a beacon that casts light far into the community and beyond, inspiring acts of contribution, compassion, and positive change. This vibrancy of character, rooted in a solid sense of self-worth, propels individuals to extend themselves beyond the confines of personal gain, reaching out to uplift others and imprinting the world with the indelible mark of their presence.

Contributing involves recognizing that each individual, buoyed by a reservoir of self-esteem, possesses a unique blend of talents, insights, and energies capable of effecting meaningful change. From the local volunteer at a community food bank whose sense of self-assurance empowers them to lead initiatives that combat hunger to the visionary entrepreneur whose confidence in their purpose drives the creation of solutions to pressing global issues, high self-esteem acts as the catalyst for action that transcends the individual, sowing seeds of progress and hope in broader fields.

Embodying the role of a positive role model emerges naturally for those whose self-esteem is deeply entrenched, for their actions, steeped in authenticity and integrity, speak louder than any words could. By simply navigating their lives with a compass of self-respect and conviction, these individuals illuminate paths for others, offering a template of living that is both aspirational and attainable. The teacher who models resilience in the face of challenges, the parent whose daily practices of kindness teach compassion, each, in their sphere, guides others towards the cultivation of their self-worth, demonstrating the profound impact of leading by example.

The legacy of kindness, a natural outgrowth of high self-esteem, flows from the understanding that recognizing one's worth does not diminish when shared with others but rather multiplies, creating an abundance that enriches all involved. Acts of kindness, whether as simple as a word of encouragement to someone struggling or as significant as dedicating one's resources to uplift a community, stem from recognizing one's capacity to contribute positively to the lives of others. This generosity of spirit, fostered by a healthy self-regard, transcends mere acts, becoming a testament to the power of self-esteem to transform the individual and the world around them.

The ripple effect of high self-esteem, manifest in every act of contribution, role modeling, and kindness, demonstrates the interconnectedness of individual well-being with the collective good. Like stones cast into a pond, the waves generated by one person's robust self-esteem extend outward, touching lives in ever-widening circles, inspiring others to recognize their value, embrace their potential, and contribute to the world in their unique ways. This cascading influence underscores the truth that building and maintaining high self-esteem is not a solitary endeavor but a communal investment with dividends that enrich the broader tapestry of human experience.

In this light, the chapters of our lives, penned with the ink of high self-esteem, contribute to a narrative much larger than our own, a narrative of collective upliftment, progress, and hope. As we turn the page from exploring the intrinsic value of self-esteem and its manifestation in personal authenticity, contribution, and kindness, we are reminded of the indelible impact our sense of self can have on the world around us. With this understanding, we step forward, not merely as individuals seeking personal fulfillment but as integral threads in the fabric of a society that thrives on its members' strength, compassion, and potential.

In closing, the journey through the realms of self-esteem, authenticity, and the legacy we leave behind serves not only as a reflection of our individual paths but as an invitation to weave our threads into the larger mosaic of human endeavor. As we move forward, let us carry with us the understanding that our sense of self-worth is both a personal beacon and a communal light, guiding our steps and illuminating the way for others.

NAVIGATING LIFE'S SEASONS

Change sweeps through our lives like the shifting winds of autumn, each gust turning the familiar into a kaleidoscope of transformation. In these moments, when the ground beneath us seems to quiver with the uncertainty of transition, our self-esteem can feel most vulnerable, most exposed to the elements. Yet, in the heart of change, it is precisely here that we find fertile soil for growth, a chance to stretch our roots deeper into the essence of who we are, even as the world around us evolves.

LIFE TRANSITIONS: MAINTAINING SELF-ESTEEM THROUGH CHANGE

Embracing Change

Change, an inevitable guest in the banquet of life, arrives at our door in myriad guises:

- A move to a new city
- The start of a new career

- The end of a relationship
- The beginning of a new chapter post-retirement

Each transition, while distinct, shares a common thread—the potential to disorient and destabilize our sense of self. To embrace change is to see it not as an intruder but as a guide, leading us toward growth. This perspective shift requires openness, a willingness to meet the unknown not with trepidation but with curiosity. Consider the act of relocating for a job. The move, fraught with the anxiety of new beginnings, also promises professional development and fresh experiences. Viewing this transition through the lens of opportunity rather than loss fosters adaptability, a crucial component in maintaining self-esteem amidst change.

Staying Grounded

In the whirlwind of change, staying grounded in one's sense of self is an anchor, steadying us against the pull of uncertainty. Strategies to maintain this grounding include regular self-reflection, a practice that allows us to reconnect with our core values and aspirations. Reflective journaling, for instance, offers a space to explore our reactions to change, question, and affirm. A prompt as simple as, "What aspects of this transition excite me? What fears arise, and how can I address them?" encourages a dialogue with oneself, fostering clarity and resilience. Maintaining routines amidst upheaval—a morning run, a nightly reading habit —also provides continuity, small islands of the familiar in a sea of change.

The Role of Support Networks

Transition periods illuminate the value of support networks, circles of empathy and understanding that encircle us with strength and encouragement. Leaning on friends, family, or community groups during times of change offers emotional solace and practical advice and assistance. Conversely, contributing to our support networks and being there for others even as we navigate our own transitions reinforces our sense of purpose and belonging. A simple act, like sharing your experience of transitioning into parenthood in a support group, not only aids in processing your own journey but also assists others, creating a reciprocally nurturing environment.

Resilience Building

Resilience, the art of rebounding from adversity, becomes a key player in life transitions. Building resilience involves cultivating a mindset equipped to face challenges with fortitude and flexibility. Practices such as mindfulness meditation and reflective journaling serve as tools in this endeavor, enhancing our awareness of the present moment and our reactions to it. When practiced regularly, mindfulness trains the mind to observe thoughts and emotions without judgment, fostering a sense of calm amid change. Coupled with journaling, which allows for externalizing and examining fears and hopes, these practices fortify our psychological resilience, enabling us to navigate transitions confidently.

Visual Element: The Transition Tree

An infographic titled "The Transition Tree" visualizes the components essential for maintaining self-esteem through change. The tree's roots represent staying grounded in one's sense of self, the trunk symbolizes the support networks that keep us steady, and the branches reaching upward embody resilience and adaptability. Leaves, scattered among the branches, bear prompts for reflection and action, such as "Identify a routine that grounds you" or "Reach out to a friend who has experienced a similar transition." This visual serves as both a reminder and a guide, illustrating the interconnected elements that support us through the seasons of change.

In navigating the seasons of life, from the flush of new beginnings to the bittersweet farewells of endings, our self-esteem is tested and fortified. By embracing change with openness, staying grounded in our sense of self, leaning on and contributing to our support networks, and building resilience, we transform the uncertainty of transition into a landscape ripe with potential. It is here, amid the flux of life's seasons, that we discover the depth of our strength and the boundless capacity for growth that resides within us.

AGING GRACEFULLY: SELF-ESTEEM IN LATER LIFE

In the infinite dance of time, aging is a serene and steady rhythm, a melody that weaves through the fabric of our existence, imbuing it with depth, texture, and color. Yet, in a society that often venerates youth and perceives aging through a lens of decline, navigating our later years with buoyant self-esteem demands resilience and a radical reimagining of what it means to grow older. This chapter invites a reflection on the beauty of aging, an exploration of the myriad ways we can counter ageism, embrace the wisdom accrued over lifetimes, maintain our physical health as a pillar of self-worth, and deliberate on the legacy we aspire to leave behind.

The specter of ageism, with its roots entangled in societal norms and stereotypes, casts long shadows across the landscape of aging, often diminishing the perceived value of older individuals. To challenge these stereotypes is to engage in an act of defiance against societal narratives that equate aging with obsolescence. This endeavor begins with acknowledging the internalized biases that shape our perceptions of aging, followed by a deliberate effort to dismantle them. Highlighting and celebrating the achievements of older individuals in various spheres—be it in art, science, activism, or everyday life—serves as a potent counter-narrative. By showcasing the diversity and richness of experiences that characterize aging, we not only refute ageist stereotypes but also elevate the discourse around aging, framing it as a phase of continued growth and contribution.

Embracing the wisdom that comes with aging is akin to uncovering a treasure trove of insights, perspectives, and knowledge amassed over decades of living. This wisdom, born of experiences both joyous and challenging, constitutes a formidable asset to self-esteem. Recognizing and valuing the wisdom of older individuals not only enriches their sense of self-worth but also fortifies the social fabric, creating a culture where the insights of older people are seen as invaluable resources. Intergenerational dialogues, mentorship programs, and platforms for older individuals to share their stories and wisdom serve as vital conduits for this exchange, bridging gaps and fostering understanding across age groups.

Physical health, a cornerstone of well-being at any age, assumes a nuanced significance in later life. Maintaining physical health in one's later years is not a pursuit of the impossible standards of youth but a celebration of the body's journey, marked by resilience and strength. Maintaining physical health includes:

- Regular, moderate exercise tailored to one's abilities.
- A balanced diet rich in nutrients.
- Regular medical check-ups to monitor and manage health conditions.

Equally important is cultivating a positive body image, an acceptance and appreciation of the body's changes as natural and worthy of respect. This holistic approach to health fosters robust self-esteem, supporting individuals in navigating the physical aspects of aging with dignity and confidence.

Considering the legacy one wishes to leave behind opens a window into the soul, revealing what individuals value most deeply. In this context, legacy transcends material inheritance, embodying instead the intangible gifts of knowledge, love, values, and memories bestowed upon those who follow in our footsteps. Crafting a legacy involves deliberate reflection on the impact we wish to have on our families, communities, and the world at large. It might manifest in sharing stories and wisdom with younger generations, the pursuit of passions that inspire others, acts of service that sow seeds of kindness, or the creation of art that captures the essence of our experiences. Through these endeavors, we not only etch our presence into the continuum of time but also reinforce our self-esteem, secure in the knowledge that our lives have meaning and purpose that endure beyond the temporal bounds of existence.

In the serene twilight of life, as we sift through the tapestry of years woven with threads of joy, sorrow, triumph, and loss, the journey of aging gracefully unfolds not as a path to be traversed with trepidation but as an odyssey to be embraced with openness and joy. This chapter, far from a mere exploration of aging, is an invitation to view the later years as a canvas awaiting the brushstrokes of wisdom, health, and legacy, a period of life abundant with opportunities for growth, contribution, and the deepening of self-esteem.

OVERCOMING LOSS AND GRIEF: THE ROLE OF SELF-COMPASSION

In the quiet aftermath of loss, once vibrant and teeming with possibility, the world often takes on a muted pallor, as if draped in a veil of silence. With its cold hands, grief carves hollow in our hearts, leaving us to navigate a landscape irrevocably altered. The shadow it casts upon self-esteem is profound, eroding the shores of our self-regard with relentless tides of sorrow and doubt. Yet, within this terrain of desolation, there lies a path lined with the tender blooms of self-compassion, a route that winds through the heart of our pain, offering solace and renewal.

Navigating the labyrinth of grief demands that we first recognize the legitimacy of our suffering, understanding that the depth of our sorrow mirrors the depth of our love and connection lost. This acknowledgment does not weaken us; rather, it affirms the richness of our human experience, validating our right to mourn. The process of grieving, often messy and nonlinear, challenges the very foundations upon which we've built our self-esteem, confronting us with questions of worthiness in the absence of those we've loved. In the raw openness of our wounds, it is here that the practice of self-compassion becomes a beacon, guiding us gently toward healing.

Self-compassion acts as a balm in these moments of vulnerability, soothing the rough edges of our pain with whispers of kindness and understanding. Its practice begins with the simple yet profound act of treating ourselves with the same empathy and care we would offer a dear friend in distress. This might manifest in allowing ourselves the grace to cry, to rage, to sit in silence without the harsh judgments that often accompany expressions of vulnerability. Mindful self-compassion exercises, such as placing a hand over the heart and speaking words of comfort to oneself, anchor us in the present, acknowledging our pain while gently encouraging a perspective of kindness and patience towards our healing journey.

The quest for meaning in the wake of loss emerges as a vital step in navigating grief, a process that seeks not to diminish our pain but to weave it into the larger tapestry of our lives. This search for significance, often a deeply personal endeavor, invites us to reflect on the impact and legacy of those we've lost, finding ways to honor their memory through our actions and choices. It might involve dedicating time to causes they were passionate about, adopting a trait or practice they embodied, or simply carrying forward the love they shared with us. In finding meaning, we transform our grief into a tribute, a testament to the enduring influence of our loved ones on our lives and selves.

Rebuilding self-esteem in the aftermath of loss is akin to nurturing a garden after a harsh winter, a gradual process of tending and care that beckons life back to barren soil. Connection, reflection, and self-care emerge as the pillars of this restoration. Engaging with supportive communities, whether through bereavement groups, friendships, or therapy, provides a space where our grief can be witnessed and held with compassion, reminding us that we are not alone in our journey. Reflective practices, such as journaling or art, offer a conduit for processing our emotions, allowing us to explore and express our grief in ways that words alone might not capture. Above all, prioritizing self-care—be it through nourishing our bodies, seeking moments of joy and relaxation, or simply permitting ourselves to rest—reaffirms our worth and nurtures our capacity to heal.

In the tender terrain of loss and grief, where sorrow carves canyons in our hearts, the practice of self-compassion lights our way, offering solace and strength. It invites us to treat ourselves with kindness, to seek meaning in our pain, and to gently rebuild the pillars of our self-esteem upon a foundation of love and remembrance. As we navigate this path, marked by the echoes of our loss, we learn that healing does not mean forgetting but rather carrying forward, bearing our scars as testaments to our capacity for love, resilience, and renewal.

SELF-ESTEEM AND PARENTING: RAISING THE NEXT GENERATION

In the intricate dance of life, the role of parenting unfurls as a tapestry rich with challenges, joys, and profound responsibilities. At the heart of this dynamic lies the nurturing of self-esteem, a foundational pillar upon which children build their understanding of themselves and their place in the world. This nurturing process, delicate and deliberate, requires more than mere intention; it demands an active engagement with practices that foster self-respect, autonomy, and a robust sense of self-worth in our children.

Modeling Self-Esteem

Modeling healthy self-esteem for our offspring mirrors the nuanced art of reflection, where children, in their observant curiosity, mirror the attitudes and behaviors they see in their guardians. This mirroring, potent in its capacity to shape perceptions and behaviors, underscores the pivotal role parents play in exemplifying self-esteem. Demonstrating self-respect, engaging in self-care, and navigating challenges with resilience offer our children a living blueprint of how to value themselves. This demonstration extends beyond the realm of actions into the domain of language, where the words we choose to describe ourselves and our experiences either fortify or undermine our self-worth. In choosing words that reflect self-compassion and understanding, we impart a lesson in subtle and profound self-esteem, teaching our children to speak to and about themselves with kindness and respect.

Encouraging Autonomy

Fostering children's autonomy is a testament to our belief in their capabilities and judgment. This encouragement, far from a laissez-faire approach, involves guiding our children toward self-sufficiency while providing the safety net of our support. It manifests in allowing them the freedom to make choices appropriate to their age and understanding, affirming their ability to navigate their world. This practice, whether it involves selecting their clothing, managing their time for homework, or choosing extracurricular activities, cultivates a sense of responsibility and decision-making that is integral to self-esteem. Encouraging autonomy also means embracing the inevitability of mistakes and viewing them as invaluable opportunities for learning rather than occasions for censure. In this environment, children learn to trust their abilities and approach life with a mindset that values growth and resilience.

Positive Reinforcement

The role of positive reinforcement in building children's self-esteem is akin to the sunlight that nurtures seedlings: essential and transformative. This reinforcement, however, extends beyond the mere acknowledgment of achievements to encompass the recognition of effort, perseverance, and the courage to try. Celebrating these qualities, irrespective of the outcome, instills a sense of worth that is not contingent on external measures of success but rooted in the intrinsic value of their endeavors. Positive reinforcement also involves highlighting each child's unique attributes and strengths, affirming their individuality and the contributions they bring to their community. By focusing our reinforcement on the process rather than solely on the results, we cultivate an environment where self-esteem thrives on a foundation of self-acceptance and appreciation for one's efforts and qualities.

Open Communication

Establishing open, honest communication with our children is the cornerstone upon which trust and mutual respect are built. This communication, characterized by active listening and empathy, creates a safe space for our children to express their thoughts, feelings, and experiences without fear of judgment. It involves engaging with their perspectives with genuine interest and offering guidance that respects their developing autonomy. Open communication also means being transparent about our challenges and vulnerabilities, demonstrating that seeking help and expressing emotions are signs of strength, not weakness. Through these exchanges, we foster a deeper connection with our children and encourage the development of their emotional intelligence, a critical component of self-esteem.

Nurturing our children's self-esteem is both an art and a responsibility. We weave together the threads of modeling, autonomy, positive reinforcement, and open communication into a tapestry that supports their growth into self-assured, resilient individuals. This nurturing process, reflective of our deepest hopes for our children's well-being, lays the groundwork for a lifetime of self-respect, courage, and fulfillment.

As we conclude this exploration of self-esteem's role in parenting, we are reminded of our actions' interconnectedness and their impact on the next generation. By modeling healthy self-esteem, encouraging autonomy, providing positive reinforcement, and maintaining open communication, we contribute to a legacy of self-worth that extends far beyond our individual lives, influencing the fabric of society itself.

EVOLVING SELF: THE TAPESTRY OF SELF-DISCOVERY

A t first glance, a single leaf might seem a mere participant in the grander canopy. Yet, each twist, turn, and vein tells a tale of growth, adaptation, and resilience. So, too, does the evolving self stand—a testament to the layers of discovery and transformation that texture the human experience. This unfolding process, nuanced and deeply personal, mirrors the intricate dance between identity and evolution, where each step forward invites a deeper understanding of who we are and who we aspire to become.

THE EVOLVING SELF: ADAPTING TO NEW SELF-DISCOVERIES

Continuous Self-Discovery

Life, in its relentless flux, presents a mosaic of experiences, each holding the potential to unveil facets of ourselves previously unexplored. This perpetual unveiling is not a task to be completed but a rhythm to be lived—a melody that harmonizes the known with the mystery of the yet-to-be-discovered. The process of self-discovery does not cease with the closing of adolescence but threads through the fabric of our entire lives, inviting us to remain open to the ever-emerging aspects of our being. Consider the moment when a passion, once dormant, stirs to life in the wake of an unexpected encounter, be it through a book, conversation, or solitary moment of contemplation. This subtle yet profound awakening prompts a reevaluation of self-concept, urging integration of this newfound passion into the narrative of identity.

Adapting to Change

Adaptation, the silent whisper behind evolution, nudges us towards acceptance and growth in the face of new self-discoveries. It beckons us to meet ourselves anew, to renegotiate our self-concept with grace and a willingness to embrace the unfamiliar. Strategies to facilitate this adaptation include cultivating a mindset that views change as an ally rather than an adversary, a perspective shift that fosters resilience and openness. Engaging in reflective practices, such as journaling or mindfulness, offers a space to explore and reconcile these changes, promoting a dialogue between the evolving self and the constants that anchor us.

Integrating New Aspects

Integrating new aspects of our identity demands a delicate balance between preservation and transformation, a dance between holding on and letting go. This integration is akin to weaving a new thread into an existing tapestry—mindfully selecting its color, texture, and placement to complement and enrich the overall pattern. Practical steps for this integration include setting aside time for introspection to understand how these emerging facets interact with and enhance our existing self-concept and employing visual or textual aids, such as vision boards or personal manifestos, to externalize and solidify this expanded sense of self.

The Importance of Flexibility

Flexibility in our self-perception and self-esteem acts as the undercurrent that allows for seamless adaptation and integration. It empowers us to meet the ebb and flow of self-discovery with poise, ensuring that our self-esteem is not tethered to rigid constructs but is fluid, capable of expanding and contracting as we evolve. Cultivating flexibility involves:

- Practicing self-compassion.
- Allowing ourselves the grace to evolve without judgment.
- Adopting a growth mindset that views personal evolution as a series of opportunities rather than obstacles.

Visual Element: The Self-Discovery Spiral

A meticulously crafted infographic, "The Self-Discovery Spiral," visually encapsulates the journey of continuous self-discovery and adaptation. Unlike a circle that returns to its beginning, this spiral represents the forward motion of growth, with each loop marking a phase of discovery, adaptation, integration, and renewed flexibility. Along the spiral, key prompts invite reflection, such as "What new aspect of myself have I uncovered recently?" and "How can I weave this discovery into the fabric of my identity?" This visual element, both a guide and a mirror, illuminates the path of evolving self-esteem, encouraging readers to embrace the beauty and complexity of their personal evolution.

In this tapestry of self-discovery, where each thread contributes to the richness of our being, we find not a destination but a journey—a continuous unfolding that reveals the depth, resilience, and adaptability of the human spirit. Through continuous self-discovery, adaptation, integration, and the cultivation of flexibility, we navigate the waters of personal evolution, steering towards a self-esteem that reflects the full spectrum of our experiences and aspirations.

FUTURE YOU: SETTING INTENTIONS FOR CONTINUED GROWTH

In the quiet moments that precede the arrival of dawn, when the world still slumbers in anticipation of the day's unfurling, a space for contemplation emerges—a sanctuary where the whispers of the future self can be heard. Within this sanctuary, envisioning the future becomes not merely an exercise in imagination but a sacred dialogue with the potential that resides within, a conversation that bridges the present with the possibilities that lie ahead. This visioning requires a departure from the familiarity of the now, an audacious step into the realm of what could be, armed with the belief in our capacity to mold our destiny with the clay of our aspirations, values, and dreams.

Visioning the Future

Envisioning the future self demands a canvas as vast as the night sky, a tableau unbounded by the constraints of current reality, upon which the hues of hope, ambition, and longing can be painted. It is an invitation to dream with audacity, to imagine oneself adorned with the qualities, experiences, and wisdom yearned for. This act of visioning transcends mere daydreaming; it is an intentional construction of a beacon that guides our choices, actions, and paths. To envision oneself with enhanced self-esteem, flourishing in well-being, and thriving in personal growth, is to lay the foundation stones for the tower of the future self. It involves exploring questions that probe the depths of our desires: "In what ways do I wish to grow?" "What strengths do I aspire to cultivate?" "How do I envision my relationship with myself and others?"

Through this inquiry, a portrait of the future self begins to emerge, a lodestar that illuminates the journey forward.

Setting Intentions

With the vision of the future self as our compass, the setting of intentions becomes the wind that propels our sails toward that envisioned horizon. Intentions, rooted in the fertile ground of our deepest aspirations, serve as declarations of our commitment to growth. They are our promises to ourselves, which bind our present actions to our future aspirations. Setting intentions is an art, a delicate balance between ambition and attainability, requiring clarity, specificity, and alignment with our core values. It is a practice that transforms the abstract into the tangible, translating the vision of the future self into actionable commitments. These intentions, whether they pertain to nurturing kindness within, cultivating resilience, or fostering connections that enrich the soul, become the guiding principles by which we navigate the terrain of personal growth.

Actionable Steps

The journey from intention to realization is paved with actionable steps, each a deliberate stride toward the embodiment of the future self. These steps, marked by intentionality and purpose, translate our aspirations into the language of reality. Formulating actionable steps requires an understanding that growth is cumulative, resulting from small, consistent actions rather than grand, sporadic gestures. It involves breaking down intentions into manageable tasks, setting milestones that mark progress, and identifying resources that support our journey. For instance, if the intention is to foster a deeper sense of self-compassion, actionable steps might include:

- Daily practices of mindfulness.
- The cultivation of a gratitude journal.
- The pursuit of activities that nourish the soul.

This systematic approach ensures that each step, no matter how small, is imbued with purpose, propelling us closer to realizing our envisioned future.

Reflecting and Revising

As we tread the path toward the future self, periodic reflection becomes our compass, ensuring that our course remains true to our envisioned destination. This reflection is a moment of pause, a time to assess the alignment between our actions and our intentions, to celebrate the milestones achieved, and to recalibrate our strategies in the face of obstacles. It acknowledges that the journey of growth is dynamic and subject to the shifting landscapes of life, and thus, our intentions and actions must be adaptable and capable of evolving in response to new insights and circumstances. Revising our intentions is not an admission of failure but a testament to our commitment to growth, recognizing that flexibility and resilience are the hallmarks of a journey marked by authenticity and purpose. Through this cycle of action, reflection, and revision, we navigate the currents of change, steering toward the future self with a spirit of exploration, determination, and grace.

THE ROLE OF TECHNOLOGY IN FUTURE SELF-ESTEEM PRACTICES

Digital Wellness

In an era where screens serve as the portals to our social, professional, and personal worlds, digital wellness emerges not merely as an advisable pursuit but as a crucial scaffold supporting the edifice of our self-esteem. This equilibrium, delicate in its composition, demands an acute awareness of how our digital engagements sculpt the contours of our self-perception, often in ways subtle yet profound. In navigating this digital landscape, cultivating practices that ensure our interactions enhance rather than erode our sense of self becomes imperative. Curating our digital consumption to align with content that uplifts and educates rather than diminishes and distracts is akin to pruning a garden, ensuring that what grows within the confines of our screens nourishes our roots of self-worth. Moreover, recognizing the signs of digital fatigue—be it through the lens of emotional exhaustion or a sense of disconnection from our physical reality—signals the need for recalibration, for moments of unplugging that allow our senses to reacquaint themselves with the richness of the world beyond pixels and notifications.

Technological Tools

Amidst the din of digital offerings, a suite of tools and applications stands ready to serve as allies in fortifying our self-esteem. These technological companions, ranging from mindfulness apps that guide us through meditations and breathing exercises to platforms that facilitate the tracking of personal achievements and goals, offer a conduit through which technology acts not as a detractor but as a bolster to our sense of self. Envision, for instance, is an application that transcribes the chaos of our thoughts into structured journals, providing clarity and insight, or a tool that, through gentle reminders, encourages the practice of gratitude, anchoring us in the present and fostering a mindset of abundance. The judicious selection of these tools, tailored to our unique paths of growth and self-care, transforms our digital devices from mere vessels of distraction into instruments of empowerment, each interaction a step toward heightened self-awareness and esteem.

Setting Boundaries

The sanctity of our digital wellness hinges upon establishing boundaries and distinctions that delineate the contours of healthy engagement. These boundaries, personal in their definition, serve as bulwarks against the tide of information and interaction that threatens to inundate our senses, safeguarding our time, attention, and energy. Establishing these limits involves an honest appraisal of our digital habits, discerning which activities replenish our spirits and which deplete them. It might manifest in designated tech-free hours, where the digital world is held at bay to allow for immersion in the physical or conscious choice to engage with social media through a lens of intention rather than compulsion. This practice of boundary setting, though requiring discipline, reclaims our autonomy over our digital lives, ensuring that our engagements uplift rather than undermine our self-esteem.

The Future of Connection

As we stand on the precipice of technological evolution, peering into the horizon where virtual and augmented realities promise to further blur the lines between the digital and the physical, speculation abounds on the future contours of connection. This frontier, vast in its potential, beckons with promises of deeper, more immersive ways of relating to one another and to ourselves. Imagine a realm where virtual support groups provide solace and solidarity across continents, where augmented reality applications offer experiences that enhance our empathy, understanding, and self-reflection. Yet, within this vision lies a caveat—a reminder that the essence of connection, fostered through pixels or presence, remains rooted in authenticity, empathy, and mutual respect. The challenge and opportunity before us is to harness these advancing technologies not as replacements for genuine human interaction but as extensions. These platforms transcend physical limitations to deepen the ties that bind us to one another and our evolving selves. As we navigate this digital dawn, our compass must remain fixed on the principles of digital wellness, ensuring that as we venture into new realms of connection, we carry with us the values that nurture and sustain our self-esteem.

GLOBAL SELF-ESTEEM: CULTIVATING COLLECTIVE CONFIDENCE

In the intricate web of global society, where threads of individual lives interlace, the fabric of collective self-esteem emerges as a pivotal determinant of the health and vibrancy of communities far and wide. This collective confidence, a reflection of the aggregated self-perceptions within a society, serves as both a mirror and a mold, shaping and being shaped by its environment's cultural, social, and economic contours. Recognizing the significance of this symbiotic relationship necessitates exploring the mechanisms through which societies can nurture a robust collective self-esteem, fostering environments where individuals and communities coexist and thrive in mutual respect and understanding.

The canvas of collective self-esteem is textured by each community's myriad cultural contributions to the global mosaic. These contributions, rich in diversity and depth, offer a palette that societies can draw to paint a picture of worldwide understanding and shared human experience. In celebrating these cultural offerings, from the arts and literature to traditions and customs, societies weave threads of appreciation and recognition into the global tapestry, enhancing the collective esteem. This celebration transcends mere acknowledgment, evolving into an active engagement with and appreciation for each culture's unique stories, histories, and perspectives. Such engagement, facilitated through festivals, educational exchanges, and media representation, enriches the global narrative and reinforces the value and worth of diverse cultural identities, contributing to a more cohesive and empathetic world community.

In the quest for a fortified global self-esteem, the pursuit of inclusivity stands as a cornerstone. This endeavor, marked by a commitment to understanding, acceptance, and respect, demands intentionally dismantling the barriers that divide. Strategies to foster inclusivity span from policy reforms that ensure equal representation and opportunities across cultural lines to grassroots initiatives that facilitate intercultural dialogue and collaboration. Though varied in scope and scale, these efforts share a common aim: to cultivate environments where differences are tolerated and celebrated as essential elements of the collective whole. In this light, inclusivity becomes not an end goal but a continuous process, a dynamic and adaptive approach to building societies where every individual, irrespective of cultural background, feels valued, heard, and empowered.

The role of education in this endeavor cannot be overstated. As a conduit for knowledge, empathy, and critical thinking, education can mold minds receptive to the nuances of global citizenship. Integral to this educational mandate is incorporating curricula that transcend traditional boundaries, offering learners insights into peoples' cultures, challenges, and contributions worldwide. Through this expansive lens, students are equipped with knowledge and the capacity for empathy, a prerequisite for the cultivation of a collective confidence rooted in mutual respect and understanding. Moreover, education emphasizing critical thinking and media literacy empowers individuals to navigate the complexities of global narratives, discerning the threads of truth and fostering an informed and thoughtful global citizenry.

As the chapter unfurls towards its culmination, reflecting on the interconnectedness that underpins our global society is imperative. The cultivation of collective self-esteem, through the celebration of cultural contributions, the fostering of inclusivity, and the role of education, emerges as a tapestry woven with the threads of individual and communal efforts. This vibrant and dynamic tapestry encapsulates the potential for societies that not only recognize but embrace the strength inherent in diversity. It envisions a world where collective confidence is a foundation for mutual respect, understanding, and collaboration across the myriad divides that have historically separated us. In this vision lies not just the aspiration for a more cohesive global community but the recognition of the indelible impact of collective self-esteem on the health, well-being, and vibrancy of societies worldwide.

As we transition from the exploration of collective self-esteem to the horizons that await, we carry with us the understanding that the hands of every individual, community, and nation continuously weave the fabric of our global society. Each thread, unique in its color and texture, contributes to the strength and beauty of the whole, a reminder of our shared responsibility and potential to foster a world marked by respect, understanding, and collective confidence.

CONCLUSION

As we draw the curtains on this transformative journey through "Rise and Shine: A Woman's Blueprint for High Self-Esteem," I find myself reflecting on the essence of our shared exploration. At the heart of this odyssey lies a core message of empowerment: high self-esteem is not a distant dream but a tangible reality attainable for every woman. By embracing inner strength, practicing diligent self-care, setting unyielding boundaries, overcoming the shadows of negative self-talk, and building nurturing communities, we unlock the door to a life of authenticity and fulfillment.

Our journey from understanding the foundational aspects of self-esteem to weaving daily practices into the fabric of our lives underscores the evolution from self-awareness to self-empowerment. The significance of navigating life's myriad challenges with resilience and fostering connections that feed our souls cannot be overstated. Each chapter, each section, has been a stepping stone towards consolidating the key takeaways that form the pillars of high self-esteem.

To you, the reader, embarking on this unique path, remember: the road to high self-esteem is personal and beautifully nonlinear. Each step, stumble, and stride forward should be celebrated as a testament to your individuality and strength. I urge you to take action and implement the strategies and practices we've discussed. Start small, embrace patience, and extend compassion to yourself as you navigate this journey.

Let us look forward with optimism. The challenges we encounter are not insurmountable obstacles but opportunities for growth, each one affirming our ability to rise, shine, and live our truth. I invite you to join the vibrant community of women who share this path. Whether through social media, online forums, or local groups, there is a wealth of shared experience and wisdom waiting to be tapped.

Remember, the quest for high self-esteem is a lifelong journey. I encourage you to continue seeking, learning, and growing. There is an abundance of resources out there—books, workshops, therapy—all designed to support you in your ongoing exploration of self.

As we part ways, I leave you with this empowering thought: You possess an inherent worth that no circumstance or challenge can diminish. Your journey of self-discovery and growth is a testament to your resilience and strength. The future is bright, illuminated by the light of your own making. Continue to rise and shine, for your presence makes the world richer.

With all my heart, I wish you courage, joy, and an unwavering belief in your own worth.

Rise and shine, for your journey is only just beginning.

KEEPING THE GAME ALIVE

Now that you've discovered the keys to boosting your self-esteem, it's time to share your newfound insights and guide others toward the same transformative journey.

By sharing your honest thoughts about this book on Amazon, you'll not only direct others who are seeking to enhance their self-worth but also pass along the torch of empowerment and self-discovery.

Thank you for your invaluable support. The journey of building high self-esteem continues to thrive because of individuals like you who choose to share their knowledge and experiences.

Your contribution helps keep this vital conversation alive, assisting me in reaching and uplifting more people just like you.

Just scan the QR code below to leave your review:

Together, we're not just reading about change; we're leading it. Thank you for being an essential part of this movement toward greater self-esteem and personal fulfillment.

REFERENCES

Self-Esteem | SpringerLink https://link.springer.com/10.1007/978-3-319-24612-3_1169

Self-esteem and brain: A social neuroscience approach https://journal.psych.ac.cn/xlkxjz/EN/abstract/abstract3770.shtml

Culture influences young people's self-esteem: Fulfillment of value priorities of other individuals important to youth https://www.sciencedaily.com/releases/2014/02/140224081027.htm

Self-worth isn't an inside job: how a narrative therapist tackles feeling worthless https://mimkempson.medium.com/self-worth-isnt-an-inside-job-how-a-narrative-therapist-tackles-feeling-worthless-f9b6dd5c4884

The relationship between family functioning and self ... https://www.ncbi.nlm.nih.gov/pmc/articles/PMC4462064/

Social Media's Effect on Self-Esteem: How Does It Affect ... https://socialmediavictims.org/mental-health/self-esteem/

Toxic Friendship: 24 Signs, Effects, and Tips - Healthline https://www.healthline.com/health/toxic-friendships

Self-Esteem and Relationships: How One Affects the Other https://psychcentral.com/lib/self-esteem-makes-successful-relationships

How solitude boosts wellbeing - University of Reading https://www.reading.ac.uk/news/2023/Research-News/How-solitude-boosts-wellbeing

Mindful Eating: Benefits, Challenges, and Strategies | USU https://extension.usu.edu/nutrition/research/mindful-eating

10 Ways to Integrate Self Care into Your Daily Routine https://www.huntingforgeorge.com/blog/10-ways-to-integrate-self-care-into-your-daily-routine/

Physical activity and self-esteem: testing direct and indirect ... https://www.ncbi.nlm.nih.gov/pmc/articles/PMC5068479/

Setting Healthy Boundaries in Relationships - HelpGuide.org https://www.helpguide.org/articles/relationships-communication/setting-healthy-boundaries-in-relationships.htm

The Impact of Social Media On Self-Esteem And Body Image https://www.impossiblepsychservices.com.sg/our-resources/articles/2023/11/15/the-impact-of-social-media-on-self-esteem-and-body-image

How to Do a Digital Detox Without Unplugging Completely https://www.everydayhealth.com/emotional-health/how-to-do-a-digital-detox-without-unplugging-completely/

Five Ways To Be Assertive At Work As A Woman https://www.forbes.com/sites/forbescoachescouncil/2022/11/02/five-ways-to-be-assertive-at-work-as-a-woman/

The Toxic Effects of Negative Self-Talk https://www.verywellmind.com/negative-self-talk-and-how-it-affects-us-4161304

How to Practice Self-Compassion: 8 Techniques and Tips https://positivepsychology.com/how-to-practice-self-compassion/

How Mindfulness Improves Self Esteem https://www.peacefullivingmentalhealth-counseling.com/post/how-mindfulness-improves-self-esteem

Fear of Failure (Atychiphobia): Causes & Treatment https://my.clevelandclinic.org/health/diseases/22555-atychiphobia-fear-of-failure

20 Ways to Overcome Perfectionism and Embrace ... https://medium.com/@wilsonisalu/20-ways-to-overcome-perfectionism-and-embrace-imperfection-b0d6561fbb1a

22+ Real Life Stories of Resilience to Empower You ... https://dailyinspiredlife.com/22-real-life-stories-of-resilience-to-empower-you-through-adversity/

Tired of playing it safe? Learn how to take risks that pay off https://www.betterup.com/blog/how-to-take-risks

Breaking down barriers: The importance of women's networks https://www.responsible-investor.com/breaking-down-barriers-the-importance-of-womens-networks/

How to Find a Mentor: 7 Easy Steps https://www.tonyrobbins.com/personal-growth/how-to-get-a-mentor/

Why Women-Centric Online Communities Are A Big Deal https://www.womenentre-preneurindia.com/viewpoint/experts-column/why-womencentric-online-communities-are-a-big-deal-nwid-200.html

Positive relationships boost self-esteem, and vice versa https://www.apa.org/news/press/releases/2019/09/relationships-self-esteem

Learn to Communicate Authentically - ALIS https://alis.alberta.ca/succeed-at-work/make-your-work-life-more-satisfying/learn-to-communicate-authentically/

Fear of judgement: why we are afraid of being judged https://nesslabs.com/fear-of-judgement

Assertive Vs Aggressive - Counseling, Therapy and ... https://www.lodestonecenter.com/assertive-vs-aggressive/

Seven Conflict Resolution Tips for Couples | National University https://www.nu.edu/blog/seven-conflict-resolution-tips-for-couples/

200 Daily Positive Affirmations For Women To Boost Self ... https://www.mental-help.net/blogs/200-daily-positive-affirmations-for-women/

Exploring Mindfulness in Relation with Self-esteem and ... https://www.ncbi.nlm.nih.gov/pmc/articles/PMC8808471/

150 Journaling Prompts for Mental Health - Journey Blog https://blog.journey.cloud/150-journaling-prompts-for-mental-health-a-comprehensive-guide-to-mindful-expression/

How Gratitude Changes You and Your Brain https://greatergood.berkeley.edu/article/item/how_gratitude_changes_you_and_your_brain

Self-Exploration: Benefits and Tips for Getting Started https://psychcentral.com/blog/self-exploration-getting-to-know-thyself

The Silent Struggle of Societal Pressures on Women's ... https://www.linkedin.com/pulse/beneath-surface-silent-struggle-societal-pressures-womens-shanker

6 Ways to Live an Authentic Life - Psych Central https://psychcentral.com/lib/ways-of-living-an-authentic-life

50 Women Who Are Changing The World Today https://motivationalspeakersagency.co.uk/news/women-who-are-changing-the-world

Life transitions and mental health in a national cohort of ... https://pubmed.ncbi.nlm.nih.gov/17605521/

Ten things you can learn from women's resilience that will ... https://www.un-women.org/en/news/stories/2020/5/compilation-ten-things-you-can-learn-from-womens-resilience

Women in Leadership Face Ageism at Every Age https://hbr.org/2023/06/women-in-leadership-face-ageism-at-every-age

9 Ways to Boost Your Child's Self-Esteem (for Parents) https://kidshealth.org/en/parents/boost-self-esteem.html

The Benefits of Being a Lifelong Learner - USU Extension https://extension.usu.edu/mentalhealth/articles/the-benefits-of-being-a-lifelong-learner

Embrace Adaptability for Personal Growth https://www.linkedin.com/pulse/like-water-art-adaptability-personal-growth-jan-sargent-p2ycf

Digital Well-being Through the Use of Technology–A ... https://www.ncbi.nlm.nih.gov/pmc/articles/PMC9853475/

The Relationship Between Collective Self-Esteem ... https://www.ncbi.nlm.nih.gov/pmc/articles/PMC4941103/

Made in the USA
Columbia, SC
14 August 2024

40496755R00089